Cherry Blossom in the Weald

THE CREAM OF KENT

★

MARCUS CROUCH

ARTHUR J. CASSELL
SHEERNESS

ISBN 0 903253 01 1

First published in 1973
by Arthur J. Cassell Ltd,
31 Broadway, Sheerness, Kent

Printed by Whitstable Litho, Straker Brothers Ltd

CONTENTS

INDEX OF ILLUSTRATIONS

COMPILED AND DRAWN BY JILL M. BOORMAN

KENT
SCALE: 9 MILES TO 1 INCH
Eastchurch
Harty
Teynham
FAVERSHAM
Ospringe
Hernhill
Boughton under Blean
Blean
Dunkirk
Whitstable
HERNE BAY
Reculver
Birchington
MARGATE
Isle of Thanet
Broadstairs
St. Nicholas at Wade
Minster
RAMSGATE
R. Stour
Stourmouth
Richborough
Fordwich
Harbledown
CANTERBURY
Wickhambreux
Littlebourne
Ash
SANDWICH
Throwley
Chartham
Chilham
Patrixbourne
Bridge
Bishopsbourne
Wingham
Eastry
Chillenden
Godmersham
Lower Hardres
DEAL
Knowlton
Challock
Boughton Aluph
Crundale
Upper Hardres
Barfreston
Walmer
Westwell
Eastwell
Wye
Waltham
Barham
Waldershare
Kingsdown
Hothfield
Denton
Coldred
St. Margaret at Cliffe
Brook
Elham
Swingfield
Hinxhill
Brabourne
ASHFORD
Alkham
Great Chart
Acrise
Lyminge
DOVER
Mersham
Paddlesworth
Postling
Stanford
Aldington
Westenhanger
Newington
FOLKESTONE
Bilsington
Warehorne
Saltwood
Newchurch
Lympne
HYTHE
Royal Military Canal
Ivychurch
Dymchurch
St. Mary in the Marsh
Brookland
New Romney
Old Romney
Lydd
Dungeness

INTRODUCTION

Not another book about Kent! It must be almost the most written-about, as well as driven-over and built-upon county in England.

There are two excuses. First, most of the existing books are either too long and bulky to make satisfactory travelling companions or too scrappy and selective to be reliable. Secondly, the reaction to scenery, buildings and antiquities is such a very personal thing that there is always room for another book which looks at this historic and beautiful county with honest and sensitive eyes. It will not tell the reader what to enjoy and find interesting, only what the writer's response is; in this way it may prove a useful yardstick by which to measure one's own reactions.

In writing about so large a county and one so packed with memories, selection cannot be avoided. Many sacrifices of places which mean much to me had to be made; even so I have exceeded the publisher's initial quota. My apologies to those villages which I have left out; I love you all!

The notes on some 220 places in Kent embody my impressions of those aspects of the countryside which especially appeal to me: the landscape, its history, its visible antiquities, its architecture, its modern developments. They are necessarily brief. The object has been to focus attention on features of interest, not to expound them. For more detail the visitor must turn to the big county histories and to the many valuable handbooks to individual churches and houses. If I have succeeded in encouraging the traveller to look around him, to travel curiously, my aim has been achieved.

Through all the centuries of recorded history Kent has been under pressure. Every invader except one landed on these shores. (The exception was William the Conqueror who chose —or the weather chose for him—the softer option of Sussex, and when he finally met the men of Kent—if we are to believe the splendid 'Invicta' legend—he put discretion before valour.) At first the pressures were from the Continent, then from a capital city bursting its seams and spilling eastwards into Kent. Now, with the Common Market and a possible Channel Tunnel, the threat to the county's integrity as well as to its peace again comes from Europe. Kent absorbed the Belgae and the Jutes, the Flemings and the Huguenots; maybe its powers of absorption are not yet exhausted. There is nevertheless no room for complacency. The title of an admirable Kentish journal is *Defend Kent*. A powerful defence lies in knowledge and understanding. The more people know and value the beauties of Kent the stronger the resistance to alien developments and indiscriminate destruction. Good hunting, then, to those who go into the lanes and the trackways which lead to the miraculously preserved heart of this lovely county.

ACRISE—*in North Downs N.W. of Folkestone.*
Really no village at all; just a manor-house and church in delectable park-land. The ancient home of the Papillon family is no longer a show-place, although it can be glimpsed from the churchyard, and the church has only rustic charms, but the setting is superb.

ADDINGTON—*in Holmesdale N.W. of Maidstone.*
Confined between M20 and A20 and so, I suppose, safe from further development. Prehistory is represented here by a fallen great-stone monument which may have been of the Coldrum type—see *Trottiscliffe*—but is now scattered beyond reconstruction. This straddles the lane which skirts Addington Park on the way to Wrotham Heath. Just off this lane to the N. are the more substantial remains of The Chestnuts, recently restored and making more sense to the untrained eye. They can be seen from the roadside. The great house of Addington Park is gone but the park remains with a footpath across it. In one corner, on a knoll which looks artificial, is the fine old church, with brasses. The village itself is set around a triangular green with a genuine—at present—village inn, The Angel. Most of the new housing is 'upper income bracket' and quite sightly. Just beyond are sand-quarries.

ALDINGTON—*in Greensand country towards Lympne.*
Here was a manor of the Archbishops, which helps to account for the magnificence of the church which stands near the old palace on a high point. The tall and majestic Tudor tower is far-seen. Inside are old choir-stalls with returns and plain misericords and a handsome Jacobean pulpit. Erasmus of Rotterdam was an absentee rector of the parish.

The straggly village is some way off along the straight road which follows the line of a Roman road out of Lympne. Some agreeable quiet country in the valley of the East Stour; a water-mill is now a show-room for antiques. On the ridge to the S. there are magnificent views—but often obscured by trees—of Romney Marsh.

ALKHAM—*in North Downs N.W. of Dover.*
Here a pretty valley gathers the head waters of the River Dour. The scenery is exceptionally fine and there are good walks—and some drives along very narrow lanes—into neighbouring valleys. The valley road itself now carries too much traffic for comfort. Alkham village is built around cross-roads, with the church up on a bank. A large and handsome building, with an Early English chapel reminiscent of Hythe. It belonged to St Radigund's Abbey—see *Poulton*.

ALLINGTON—*on Medway below Maidstone.*
Until recently there was nothing here but the castle and the church, but large estates have sprung up towards the London Road and a marina brings traffic down past the castle gate.

Here Stephen of Penchester (Penshurst) fortified a manor-house in Edward I's reign. The castle was enlarged in Tudor times when Sir Henry Wyatt reaped his reward for backing the winning side at Bosworth Field. His son Sir Thomas Wyatt was born here; he played multiple roles, as courtier, diplomat and poet, at the Court of Henry VIII and was in real peril because of youthful associations with Anne Boleyn. His son, another Thomas, led a revolt against the proposed marriage of Mary and Philip of Spain and, no doubt, against the threatened re-establishment of the monasteries—the Wyatts had acquired the lands of Boxley Abbey; he lost the gamble and his head. By the beginning of the 20th century Allington Castle had become a shabby ruin. Martin Conway (later Lord Conway of Allington) bought it and restored it to a splendour perhaps greater than it had ever known. It is now a Carmelite retreat and conference centre, and can be visited regularly.

The castle is exceedingly picturesque, especially from the river which here is most lovely. The lowest lock of the Medway Navigation is at Allington and here pleasure-boats moor in their dozens. A riverside hostelry—once a humble inn—dispenses good food.

APPLEDORE—*on edge of Romney Marsh.*

The alphabet makes this the first of my Top-Twenty of Kentish villages. The High Street is almost a miniature of Tenterden, with a strip of green, and handsome and varied houses on either side. At the foot the line is broken effectively by a projecting inn and then the main road turns abruptly over the Royal Military Canal on to the Marsh.

Appledore has an important strategic position. The Rother flowed into the marshy wastes here before the reclamation of Romney Marsh, and here begins the Rhee Wall, crossing the flats to New Romney, which was an agent in the reclamation. The modern road follows the wall closely. The village stands on a conspicuous bank which was doubtless the fortification thrown up by invading Danes in the 10th century. The Royal Military Canal follows roughly the original course of the Rother towards Lympne. The banks are in the National Trust's care and offer a delightful walk.

From the canal there is an impressive view of the church with its massive low tower. Here, among other good things, is a monument to Philip Chute, standard-bearer to Henry VIII. His home was at Horne's Place, on the lane to Kenardington. The medieval house has gone—or perhaps has had a facelift—but its exquisite domestic chapel is still there.

ASH-CUM-RIDLEY—*in North Downs beyond Wrotham Hill.*

Astonishingly lovely country so near to London. The steep dry valleys keep the scenery from monotony, and there are

New Ash Green, a new village near Ash, on Wrotham Hill

some excellent walks. Ash itself is a small village standing away from the old nucleus of hall and church. These make a pretty group in brick and flint in a setting of noble trees. A track goes off here to the neighbouring, and associated, village of Ridley where there is a similar group. The rich farmland inspired the poet and painter Thomas Hennell whose father was vicar here.

Just N. of Ash church and hall is the massive new development of New Ash Green, a 'model' planted village. This may not be to all tastes—it is not to mine—but it is at least to be preferred to the mindless straggle which seems to be the only alternative in an area which is always under urban pressure.

ASH-NEXT-SANDWICH—*between Sandwich and Wingham.*

An elongated village on the low ridge which carries the Sandwich road above the Wantsum flats. At its heart is the church, with a superb central tower and spire which can be seen for miles around. One of the finest of Kentish parish churches, a monument to the prosperity of these parts in the 13th century. Equally splendid inside, and containing some of the greatest of Kentish monuments.

The village itself suffers from incessant traffic. Consequently it is difficult to evaluate adequately the houses—some of them admirable—which line the single street.

AYLESFORD—*on the tidal Medway.*

An ancient river-crossing, long before present fine medieval stone bridge was built. Here, according to tradition, the British held the crossing against the invading Saxons under Hengest and the leader's brother Horsa was killed. The story is in detail improbable but the ford had obvious strategic importance. The old village stands on a terrace above the river, an admirable example of unconscious planning. The view downstream from the Bailey Bridge is almost the most famous scene in Kent. Finely placed church, on the highest ground, has Norman and later features. Good monuments include Culpepers from Preston Hall, in sanctuary. Holy Trinity Hospital, almshouses, recently enlarged, were founded by the Sedley family in 1605.

Downstream, on the banks of the Medway, the Friars, the site of a Carmelite house founded by a returned Crusader in 1240. It was the first home of the White Friars in England. At the Dissolution this became a mansion, of which substantial remains can be seen. In 1949 the Carmelites returned to Aylesford, and a church and other buildings have since been added. The Friars is open regularly to the public.

Kits Coty, on Bluebell Hill, Aylesford

Across the river there are industrial installations and wide acres of modern housing.

The large parish of Aylesford is rich in prehistoric remains. On the side of Blue Bell Hill, in fine open position, is Kits Coty, the most famous great-stone monument in S.E. England; exposed stone chamber of a burial mound with vast capstone. Dates from New Stone Age, say 2000 B.C. Looked after by D of E with hideous (necessary?) iron railings. Directly below is Little Kits Coty, or The Countless Stones, a similar grave-site which has collapsed into a confused heap (D of E). White Horse Stone and others, some of them natural 'sarsen' stones, in neighbourhood.

BAPCHILD—*N. Kent, near Sittingbourne.*
As usual, old village lies just off Watling Street. Spring N. of

road traditionally connected with Canterbury pilgrims. Exceptionally fine church with excellent details, notably angle piscina elegantly carved and elaborate niche in nave pillar.

BARFRESTON—*tiny village in chalk downs behind Dover.* Nothing much here except church, but this is of national importance. Perfect survival of late-Norman building, date around 1175. Fine chancel arch and much carving inside. Outside, eastern wheel-window and sculpture, priests' door, corbel table with grotesque carving (some of it modern replacement). High spot is S.W. door with rich carving. Worth an hour of anyone's time to study this and some could spend a lifetime on the task. Details include Christ in Glory (centrepiece of tympanum), archbishop? Thomas Becket in keystone, king and queen (maybe Henry II and Eleanor), creatures from

Parkland above Barham

mythology and medieval beast-legends, and contemporary humans carrying out everyday tasks. A marvellous building. Don't forget to put something in the collecting-box; it is a small parish to maintain so priceless a treasure.

BARHAM—*at foot of Elham Valley.*
Barham Downs above village was popular meeting-place for centuries. Elections held here in open air, and Charles I had picnic with his future consort while escorting her from Dover to London. Handsome mansion in park with fine trees. Copper spire of church is one landmark. The other, Barham Mill, recently destroyed by fire; the downs will never look the same again.

BARMING—*on Medway above Maidstone.*
Huge mental hospital at Oakwood; main building is goodish architecture in massive monumental manner of 1830. There were two Barmings, but West—near present house of Barnjet—has vanished, church and all. East Barming church, in orchards away from village, is pretty building with spire. Norman chancel. Best features, imported, are handsomely carved choir-stalls of 15th century date. Wooden bridge over Medway in picturesque setting; one of the best towpath walks starts here.

BAYHAM ABBEY—see *Lamberhurst.*

BEARSTED—*E. of Maidstone.*
New housing has almost linked village with Maidstone and current plans are designed to do just that. The character of the village has been radically changed, not for the better. In old village, north of main road, is splendid village green famous in cricketing history, surrounded with mainly good houses. Baroness Orczy, creator of the Scarlet Pimpernel, lived here. Handsome large church lies away on edge of village with

pleasant country beyond. Note tower with grotesque figures a-top.

BENENDEN—*Wealden village in lovely country.*
Main street is rich in varied and picturesque houses and so is the country around. One of the best village greens in Kent, backed by church and with old school building on one flank. This was founded by one of the Gibbon family, from which the historian came. The church looks better at a glance than in detail, but note salamander in boss of porch. The great house of Benenden, formerly Hemsted, seat of Earls of Cranbrook, is now well-known public school for girls; it stands in magnificent park. Near Iden Green, S. of village, there are traces of a Roman ford. Between Benenden and Cranbrook is Hemsted Forest, one of the largest of Kentish Forestry Commission plantations; many woodland walks if you don't mind the preponderance of conifers.

BENOVER—see *Yalding.*

BETHERSDEN—*between Ashford and Tenterden.*
Nobly sited church at high point of village street. The district was once noted for Bethersden marble, a limestone encrusted with shells which takes a high polish; it is much used inside Kent churches and for paving. Present industry is making of wooden 'Colt' houses.

BEULT, RIVER—*tributary of Medway.*
It drains the eastern half of the low Weald. Rises near High Halden and passes through Smarden, Headcorn and near Staplehurst before entering Medway at Yalding. Ancient bridges at Smarden (Town Bridge and Hadman's Bridge), Headcorn (Stephen Bridge), Herstfield Bridge near Cross-in-hand, and Yalding. Never a wide stream but highly picturesque

and passing through quietly attractive country throughout its course. Well worth exploring in detail.

BIDBOROUGH—*on Wealden ridge S. of Tonbridge.*
Recent building has spoilt much of its character, but the view from Bidborough Ridge is still one of the best in Kent, looking to long line of greensand and downs. Tiny church tucked away remotely, pretty rather than interesting.

BIDDENDEN—*in the Weald, between Headcorn and Tenterden.*
An early forest settlement which achieved prosperity with the boom in the cloth trade. This gave the village its present appearance, which has a greater harmony than places where the process of growth was more gradual. A lovely high street narrows towards the church which effectively closes the view. Black-and-white and red tile provide just enough variety to hold the interest. The street is paved with Bethersden marble slabs. A neat little green in the foreground holds the village sign which displays the Biddenden Maids, Siamese twins born here probably in Elizabethan times; they founded a local charity which continues. Away from the street there are some very good houses, including a great rambling cloth-hall.

The church looks exciting, with its massive tower of early Tudor date. The interest is not quite sustained inside.

BILSINGTON—*on the edge of Romney Marsh.*
A cross-road village of some charm but no great distinction. There was a small house of Augustinian canons here, of which some fragments remain in private hands. The landmark hereabouts is an obelisk on a little hill, now sadly decayed, which commemorates the death in a coach accident of a 19th century MP. Towards the Military Canal, and hidden behind a farm, is the little church, endearingly small and muddly.

BIRCHINGTON—*now a western suburb of Margate.*

A little of the old village remains in a sea of new housing and busy main roads. Here Dante Gabriel Rossetti spent his last days and is buried in the old church.

At Quex Park, to the S., marked by a curious iron structure called the Waterloo Tower, there is a Museum—the Powell-Cotton Collection—of national importance; its emphasis is on natural history. Open to the public on certain summer days.

BIRLING—*in Holmesdale, W. of Snodland.*

A straggling village in excellent country. To the N. the downs rear up in a splendid green bank affording a fine open view over the Medway valley. Just beyond the escarpment there is a sandy wooded summit called Holly Hill, in public hands, a pleasant picnic-spot and the starting-point of some of the best walks in Kent. One of these follows an ancient sunken track to Dode. This, according to a convincing tradition, was a village wiped out in the Black Death and never resettled; all that remains is a tiny two-cell Norman church, restored but still retaining its authentic atmosphere. One of the most evocative places I know. Birling belonged to the Nevill family, Earls of Abergavenny. They have gone now (their seat is at Eridge Castle, just over the border into Sussex) but the pretty and well-sited church is full of memories of them. Their arms are everywhere, on formal achievements, hatchments and a magnificent cast-iron cover to the family vault. High on the chancel wall is the tilting-helmet of Sir Edward Nevill who is said to have worn it at the Field of the Cloth of Gold (1520). At the back of the church, Royal Arms of William III.

BISHOPSBOURNE—*W. of Watling Street in the valley of the Little Stour.*

A very small village with a real personality. It sits in a corner of Bourne Park—see *Bridge*. It has a place in history as the last home of two great masters of English prose. Richard Hooker became rector here in 1595 and here completed his defence of the Church of England *Of the Laws of Ecclesiastical Polity*. A quiet saintly man forced reluctantly into the centre of national controversy. His monument stands to the S. of his altar in the pretty church. Burne Jones stained glass in W. window. In 1919 the white house Oswalds beside the church became the home of Joseph Conrad and he lived here until his death in 1924. He is buried in Canterbury.

BLEAN—*N. of Canterbury.*
Full name St Cosmus-and-St Damian-in-the-Blean. The Blean was the great forest straddling Watling Street. Long vanished, although there are still very pleasant woodlands including a nature reserve. Some agreeable walks. The little woodland church has been much restored, and there was some shabby development between the Wars, without benefit of planning.

BORDEN—*between Watling Street and M2 Motorway.*
On its northern boundary Borden merges into Sittingbourne, and a hasty glance would suggest that there is nothing of note here. There remains in fact a tiny centre which is a model of its kind. On the flat top of a little hill a fine church stands in the middle of a square. Some of the surrounding houses are worth a glance. The church is of the highest interest. Solid Norman and 13th century work with massive tower and an ornate S. porch. Lots to see inside, including an angle piscina in the N. Kentish manner (compare those at Bapchild and Hartlip) and the elaborate wall monument to Dr Robert Plot, who was the 'Hasted' of Staffordshire.

Beyond the old village suburbia ends abruptly and there are miles of fine rolling chalk country.

BOUGHTON—*four villages of this name in Kent.*

BOUGHTON UNDER BLEAN—*the great Blean Forest occupied heights above village.*

Original settlement lies to S. of Watling Street but main village lines the street, with a few excellent houses, some half-timbered, some with elegant plastered fronts. Church in very pretty setting remote from most of the houses. Chief interest lies in the collection of monuments to members of the Hawkins family and others.

BOUGHTON ALUPH—*on Pilgrims Way at entrance to Stour Gap through North Downs.*

The Way comes out of Eastwell Park and crosses fine big triangular green where cricket is played. Some pleasant modest houses in brick, notably the inn (meals). Pilgrims Way continues as lane and track to church, a massive hall-like structure with huge squat tower. This noble building plays a part in annual Stour Festival of music and art.

Boughton Malherbe Place

BOUGHTON MALHERBE—*on Greensand ridge E. of Maidstone.*

Main population at Grafty Green. The hall and church stand isolated on ridge with magnificent views. Wotton monuments in church. The Wotton mansion, much altered, was home of Thomas Wotton, statesman-manqué of Elizabeth's reign and of his son, Sir Henry, adventurer, diplomat, wit, poet and scholar—one of the most picturesque and interesting of Kentishmen. Read brief gossipy biography by Isaak Walton.

BOUGHTON MONCHELSEA—*large village on Greensand ridge S. of Maidstone.*

Village sprawls behind ridge, with pretty walks through old quarries. Here Kentish rag was taken for many famous buildings. On edge of ridge is church, of no great architectural interest after drastic restoration but commanding one of the best views in Kent. Churchyard, entered by 15th century lychgate, is a terraced garden with roses. In the foreground of view is Boughton Park with deer and noble trees, and behind the church is Boughton Place (open summer weekends) a fine late Tudor mansion. Footpath through the park follows the ridge to the Suttons, crossing at one point the line of the Roman road from Rochester to the Wealden iron workings, here a picturesque sunken track with high ragstone walls.

BOURNE PARK—see *Bridge.*

BOXLEY—*just below North Downs N.E. of Maidstone.*

Well up in my Top Twenty of Kentish villages. Small village with (so far) controlled development. Tennyson lived here. Village green has inn and church in classic rivalry. Church is very picturesque and interesting, with rare western porch, perhaps used as reliquary. Boxley was famous in Middle Ages for its abbey, whose abbot held high rank among Lords. It was severely treated at Dissolution when the Rood of Grace was exposed as a fraud (its wonder-working effigy was operated by a system of wires). Nothing much remains except great barn, broken walls and chapel-at-gate (now a cottage and former post office). The area offers some good downland walks as well as a restful low-level stroll through to Detling.

BRABOURNE—*E. of Ashford.*
Pilgrims Way (southern branch) passes nearby. Much new building but old village street is still unspoilt. At east end is church, with massive tower so low as not to be recognized by O.S. map-makers. One of best churches in Kent. Full of interest and beauty. See particularly Easter Sepulchre on N. side of altar, heart-shrine to member of Scott family, and fine Jacobean pulpit.

BRASTED—*in Holmesdale W. of Sevenoaks.*
The high street, with many houses dating from coaching days, suffers from being part of busy A25 (but relief is on the way). The White Hart was a favourite haunt of pilots from Biggin Hill in Battle of Britain, and still remembers them. Church, N. of village, largely rebuilt but interesting and well kept. Note the extraordinary buttresses of the tower. Modern glass and some nice carvings of the four Evangelists—St Luke appears as the most benign bull. Brasted Place, S. of road is large and eccentric mansion in which Adam had a hand (now a theological college).

BREDGAR—*in downs S. of Sittingbourne.*
Some dreadful new building. You see the tall church tower from the motorway but can't get to it. There was a college of priests here, of which a fragment, now called the Chantry, remains. Big church with monuments, hatchments and a barrel-organ. Some outstandingly good houses in the parish, notably Bexon (to E.) one of the best Kentish yeoman's houses to survive.

The Butcher's Shop, Brenchley

BRENCHLEY—*on Wealden ridge above Paddock Wood.* One of the best of Kentish views N. across the Medway valley. This is a most attractive village with a rich variety of houses; timber-frame, tile-hung, brick and weatherboard—the whole gamut of Kentish domestic. One spectacular black-and-white house on the main road W., and the Old Palace—now post office, etc.—is a fine range. The church faces a tiny square. An attractive, greatly restored building—the best of it is the churchyard which has an avenue of yews and flowering trees with nice views. To S. is Brattles Grange, a lovely half-timbered house with a small garden open during the summer. The district abounds in delightful houses. W. is the detached hamlet of Matfield with a large green, complete with duckpond. Behind this is a most handsome house of about 1730. Further W., on a lane leading to Capel, is Crittenden; a long tile-hung house with a famous garden, often open. N. of Matfield, overlooking the low Weald, is the house in which Siegfried Sassoon lived in the years immediately before the First World War. (The period of *Memoirs of a Fox-Hunting Man* and *The Weald of Youth*, which contain descriptions of this landscape.)

BRIDGE—*on the Dover Road E. of Canterbury.*
The bridge crosses the Little Stour in the village. Far too much traffic for comfort, and the real charms are obscured. There is a little Norman work in the church, but it is outclassed by neighbouring Patrixbourne (which may be approached most pleasantly by footpath from beside the inn). Just beyond the village Bourne Park lies towards the river, a fine landscape design in which are set Bourne Place and Bridge Place, two handsome 18th century mansions. A public road traverses the park to Bishopsbourne. There is some very beautiful country to the S.

BROADSTAIRS—*on Thanet coast.*
The best survival in the South of a Victorian watering-place. The original settlement was at St Peter's, inland, where there is a large, rather gaunt medieval church. There are brick Flemish-gabled cottages nearby. Beyond St Peter's the coast is reached at Kingsgate, where there are still some survivals of the agreeable Gothic follies put by Lord Holland in late 18th century. The unique tower of Kingsgate Castle was devised as the stables of his house.

Over Broadstairs itself brood the spirits of Queen Victoria and Charles Dickens. Victoria stayed at Pierremont House—now the Council Offices, Dickens stayed pretty well everywhere and owned Bleak House on the headland—open to the public. To these worthies is now added Edward Heath, who

Dicken's House, Broadstairs

was born here. Pleasant gardens border the cliffs of the semicircular Viking Bay, and the town is full of oddly agreeable alleys. At Joss Bay, beyond the North Foreland lighthouse, there is a sandy beach and good swimming.

BROOK—*below North Downs E. of Ashford.*
Only a single street but a pretty one. The village is dominated by the massive early Norman tower of the church, one of the best village churches in Kent. The walls of the sanctuary are covered with paintings contemporary with the fabric. They are not at first easy to decipher, but a little quiet study will reveal many exquisite pictures—the whole church was a Bible picture-book.

Next to the church is a noble barn which now houses the agricultural museum of Wye College—limited opening. Beyond the village rises the steep wall of the downs, cleft in the middle by a spectacular combe—the Devil's Kneading Trough. The downs are a National Nature Reserve, famous for orchids and other flowers of the chalk. Access is limited, but there are public footpaths and a nature trail. The view from the top is magnificent, and a walk continues E. towards Hastingleigh and Brabourne.

BROOKLAND—*on Walland Marsh.*
One of the unforgettable sights of Kent is here, the huge detached campanile of Brookland Church, a candle-snuffer in timber dating from 13th century. Many jolly stories are extant to account for it, but less picturesquely and more practically the structure distributes the weight evenly over the marshy ground. This is a church of most exceptional interest—allow at least an hour and buy a copy of the excellent church guidebook. The centre of interest is the Norman font, a great lead tub with relief decorations of the Zodiac and the occupations of the seasons—a wonderful glimpse into the everyday life of eight centuries ago.

For a view of the marsh country take a lane here which leads beside heron-haunted rhines past the lonely church of Fairfield to Appledore. If you are sensitive to the mystery of this land won from the sea, this will be a journey to remember for a lifetime. Best seen in the last sunlight of a fine Spring day.

BURHAM—*above the Medway gap.*
Cement workers deserted the old village down by the river in favour of a new settlement on the side of the downs. Here is a large, rather impressive Gothic-revival church. The old church moulders gently in the marshes where the Pilgrims Way crosses the river from Snodland. Marvellously evocative country this, with sites of Roman villas, ruins of Victorian cement

kilns, reedy streams and an abundance of birds. An old track climbs to the top of Bluebell Hill.

CANTERBURY—*city grown up where ancient trackway and later Roman Watling Street cross R. Stour.*

Permanent settlement shortly before Julius Caesar's invasion (remains of hill-top camp which preceded it at Bigbury, about two miles W. along Pilgrims Way). Capital of Roman Cantium and later of Saxon kingdom of Kent. Here in A.D. 597 Augustine set up base for conversion of the English and baptized Ethelbert King of Kent. Ethelbert's consort Queen Bertha, already Christian, had chapel outside city walls; this survives as core of Church of St Martin. Augustine founded Cathedral and also Abbey of SS Peter and Paul (later St Augustine's Abbey).

No remains of Saxon Cathedral or of successor built by first Norman Archbishop Lanfranc. Western crypt and some lower walls of choir date from rebuildings in early 12th century. After fire in 1174 choir rebuilt in revolutionary new style; this with chapels and corona to east remain, finest late 12th century work in England. Lanfranc's nave replaced in late 14th century by present Perpendicular nave. Central tower (Bell Harry Tower) finished early in Tudor age.

Canterbury's fame as seat of Primate of All England reinforced when Archbishop Thomas Becket was murdered in Cathedral in 1170 after fatal quarrel with King Henry II over church privileges. The martyr's shrine became principal objective of medieval pilgrims and the Cathedral and the city profited by their gifts. Shrine completely destroyed at Reformation (conjectural reconstruction in R.C. Church of St Thomas of Canterbury, Burgate Street; the original is illustrated several times in contemporary stained glass in Cathedral.)

The Cathedral Church of Christ was served by a Benedictine Priory of which there are very complete remains, including

Bell Harry Tower, Canterbury Cathedral

cloisters, chapter-house and water-tower. The rival abbey of St Augustine was destroyed at Dissolution except for two gatehouses and a few buildings incorporated in a royal palace. Foundations of abbey church cleared by Office of Public Buildings and Works and reveal fascinating history of building and rebuilding. Site of burial-place of Augustine, Ethelbert and other Saxon archbishops and kings. Shell of Saxon church of St Pancras to S.E.

Of the many other monastic houses in the city only a few fragments remain; refectory of Blackfriars, picturesque island-house from Grey Friars (first house of Franciscan friars in England), scrap of wall of Austin Friars preserved in car-park. Medieval almshouses, St Johns and Eastbridge still in use and may be visited.

Much of city walls remain with splendid West Gate (c. 1373). In angle of wall is Dane John, a great mound, sepulchral or defensive, of unknown date, prettified in 19th century and enclosed in attractive public-garden. Monuments here include Christopher Marlowe, born in Canterbury in 1564, and Invicta, locomotive from pioneer railway between Canterbury and Whitstable.

Some fine ancient houses survive, especially to N. and W. of Cathedral and in Precincts, but a large part of the central area was devastated in Blitz of 1942. Not everyone will like the new Canterbury built from the ruins, but there is some interesting new work between St George's Street and Burgate Street. On St Stephen's Hill to North new University buildings, including twin colleges aligned on Cathedral with magnificent views; also Gulbenkian Theatre (productions open to public). Another theatre, the Marlowe, in St Margaret's Street (near site of Roman theatre, so continuing a 1700-year-old tradition.)

CAPEL—see *Tudeley*.

St Augustine's Abbey, Canterbury. The Great Gate

CHALK—*Thamesside E. of Gravesend.*

Part of the old village is merged with the urban mass of Gravesend; then there is a thin green belt before the church is reached. Chalk cherishes memories of Dickens who spent his honeymoon here and, despite the ill-fate of his marriage, retained affection for the place. The old—and battered—forge is one of the many originals of Joe Gargery's forge in *Great Expectations.* Dickens wrote appreciatively of the grotesque carving above the W. porch of Chalk church where, below a niche vacated by Our Lady or a saint, a gross monk cuddles his pitcher of sack. The church itself stands up well with wide views to London River but has no special antiquarian interest.

CHALLOCK—*in North Downs between Charing and Canterbury.*

The motorist hell-bent for Canterbury and the Thanet coast sees only a long narrow strip of common land—the Lees—on which he is prevented from parking. A short diversion S. leads by a dead-end lane to the old church on the edge of Eastwell Park in a setting of great beauty. A track leads on through beechwoods to Eastwell Church and the Pilgrims Way. A place to linger in. The church became derelict through war-damage and disuse and might, like Eastwell, have fallen into ruin. Devoted efforts led to restoration, and it is now a building of considerable beauty. Note remains of rood screen and beam for the Lenten veil. Some nice grotesque carving outside. The high-spot is a mural in the choir by Mr John Ward, RA, a local artist of distinction. This shows the baptism of Christ in Jordan, a little Kentish stream, with the parochial church council drawn up on the opposite bank as witnesses.

Between Challock, Chilham and Boughton Aluph stretches the vast tract of Kings Wood, one of the largest national forests in Kent, with many tracks open to walkers who may be lucky enough to catch a glimpse of deer.

Winter Landscape, Chartham Down

CHARING—*below North Downs at junction of roads from Canterbury and Ashford.*

To its importance at the dividing of main routes was added the Archbishop's patronage, for the Primate owned the manor. Remains of his palace stand in picturesque decay beside the church in a charming, narrow road leading off the high street. The church has one of the best of the characteristic Kentish towers. Altogether a handsome building as befits one which enjoyed the Archbishop's favour. The village has many handsome houses in brick and timber, as well as the prettiest butcher's shop in Kent.

A windmill crowns Charing Hill, almost hidden among trees. From the main road there is a wide view over the Weald with the Fire Hills by Hastings on the skyline and to the left a glimpse of the sea. Between village and hilltop passes the Pilgrims' Way, at almost its prettiest just to the W.

CHARTHAM—*in Stour valley S. of Canterbury.*

A large scattered village dominated by the huge bulk of St Augustine's Hospital on Chartham Down. Behind this one of the loveliest roads in Kent runs across to join Stone Street. Chartham is a mixture of old and new, and unusually, some of the best houses are new—a group just behind the church. Because of the river a paper-mill was established here in the 18th century and this continues. Between Stour and Mill Stream is the big cruciform church, showing some of the best examples of 'Kentish' tracery of the late 13th century. This is a splendid building, housing, among other treasures, the magnificent brass of Sir Robert de Septvans, 1306, among the very finest in the world. There is a riverside walk from Chartham to the Canterbury road, passing on the opposite bank two tiny medieval chapels at Horton and Milton.

CHARTWELL—see *Westerham.*

CHATHAM—*on the tidal Medway.*

With the running down of the dockyard some of the heart has gone out of Chatham, but it is a busy town, improving as a shopping centre as Rochester declines. There are few visible reminders of its great days, for the docks are private, except on visitors' days. From Fort Pitt, site of one of the 19th century defences which ringed the Medway Towns, there is a good view over the town with the river twisting round upon itself. Just between here and the railway station is Ordnance Terrace, where Dickens came to live as a child and gathered some of the lasting impressions of his life. The house is in a poor state. A later home near the Town Hall has vanished. A few 18th century houses of quality survive precariously.

CHEVENING—*below North Downs N.W. of Sevenoaks.*

The modern commuter village is at Chipstead to the S. Chevening remains a tiny hamlet at the gate of Chevening Park and will, one hopes, remain so! Here about 1630 Lord Dacre built a classical mansion in Holmesdale, a pioneer building of its day. Later additions and alterations by the Earl Stanhope rather spoiled the effect. The house has associations with Pitt and with that eccentric and adventurous feminist Lady Hester Stanhope. Chevening Place is surrounded by a fine park, enclosing a mile of the Pilgrims Way so that modern pilgrims are sent around three sides of the square. At the end of the village street what was once the main London road becomes a rough and very steep track up to Knockholt.

Chevening is a highly picturesque village dominated by the church with its handsome early Tudor tower. Most notable for monuments to Lennards and Stanhopes. Exquisite Chantry monument to Lady Frederica Stanhope, 1827.

CHIDDINGSTONE—*in Weald N.W. of Penshurst.*

Only the single side of a short street but one of the most

Next page: Chevening Village

Chiddingstone Roofs

familiar and pleasing sights in Kent. The National Trust has the houses in its care; they are all different and each of its kind is excellent. Don't miss also lovely cottage, allegedly former almshouse, on footpath across the Eden. The church is an interesting oddity, being largely a Jacobean rebuilding and a good attempt at remaining true to a Gothic original.

Behind the street is the 'Chiding Stone', a natural outcrop of sandstone and nothing to do with the village name.

Chiddingstone stands in very delightful country and is the base for a number of good walks in the valley of the little River Eden.

CHILHAM—*in middle of Stour gap through the North Downs.* For most people Chilham is top of the Kentish charts, a village of almost unbelievable excellence. There is scarcely a false note anywhere, and only the visitors and their cars spoil the place. A hilltop village—now happily bypassed—set at the crossing of the Maidstone–Canterbury road with the Pilgrims Way. They meet in a small square with on two sides handsome half-timbered and brick houses, on the third the church and on the fourth the gates of Chilham Castle. It is so lovely that few visitors penetrate farther, to discover the beautiful early 18th century vicarage, Robin's Croft and other fine houses in the street, and the splendid Woolpack Inn at the foot of the hill.

The church, in chequerboard flint, is sturdy and effectively placed on the highest point. It is chiefly famous for its monuments, which exhibit most styles from Jacobean to Victorian and include a Nicholas Stone, a Chantry and a very charming study of children from mid-Victorian times—a perfect period-piece.

Of the medieval castle which guarded the river-gap only the Henry II keep remains. The rest was destroyed and the site used for a notable and eccentric mansion built in 1616. This is not open, but the gardens may be visited regularly. They are well worth seeing for their Jacobean terraces, the 18th century landscaping and the noble views across the river. On the hills opposite, below a conspicuous clump, there is a rarity for Kent, a long barrow called Jullieberries Grave. Finding it presents some difficulties, but the search will take you to delightful country with views back to the village and castle backed by the dark mass of Chilham Park.

CHILLENDEN—*in North Downs E. of Canterbury.* This is Jane Austen country; she was a regular visitor to houses at Goodnestone and Rowling. The principal interest here lies in the windmill, a post mill of the most primitive kind with open trestle. This is now publicly owned and may be visited.

CLIFFE-AT-HOO—*in Hoo peninsula between Thames and Medway.*
Sprawling, mainly unattractive village on the edge of the Thames marshes with fine bird-haunted walks to the N. The church is right on the edge of the marshes, a magnificent flint building impressive from the outside and splendid within, with fine detail of 13th and 14th centuries.

There is a notable Tudor house—Manor Farm—in West Street with the tallest of brick chimneys.

COBHAM—*to the S. of A2 W. of Rochester.*
Medieval and Tudor splendours compete with memories of Dickens. The Leather Bottle, opposite the church, is almost a Dickens museum as well as a pleasant place to eat. This was the setting of a famous scene in *Pickwick.* The village is a mixture of unobtrusively satisfactory old and mostly awful new.

The church is as notable for its architecture as for its monuments, which is saying a lot. The chancel was rebuilt in the 13th century and is enormously wide and light, with great richness of detail; look for example at the lovely canopied piscina. Cobham was dominated in the Middle Ages by the noble Cobham family, and in 1362 Sir John de Cobham founded a college of priests here and the church was again enlarged then. To the Cobhams, and their successors the Brookes, Cobham Church owes its unique possession, a matchless series of monumental brasses, incomparably the finest in existence. From 1320 to 1529 they illustrate the history of costume and armour in finest detail. Contrast with these the aggressive alabaster tomb of George Brooke, Lord Cobham,

Cobham Hall

of 1561, which stands right in front of the altar. The great lord puts the Almighty firmly in His place!

Behind the church is Cobham College, Sir John's foundation remodelled by George Brooke's son as almshouses in 1598. A pretty quadrangle, more Elizabethan than medieval, with a handsome great hall beyond—the whole faintly reminiscent of a very small Oxford college. The building still fulfils its charitable function. Visitors are welcomed.

At the E. end of the street the park of Cobham Hall stretches almost to infinity with occasional glimpses of the mansion through the trees. Park and Hall are private and the Hall is now a public school for girls, but there are footpaths through the park and the hall and its gardens may be visited during school holidays. The house was built—on the site of an older house—by the Lord Cobham who revitalized the College. It is Elizabethan work, in brick and stone, on an imposing scale. To this an even more splendid centrepiece was added in Charles II's reign, with great stone entrance and steps. There were additions later in the 18th century when Repton landscaped the park. The pleasure-gardens behind the house are charming, a grotto and mock-Neolithic great-stone monuments standing beside a classical temple with that age's cheerful disregard of historical propriety. There are enjoyable walks through the park, one of them leading to the sadly ruined mausoleum built for Lord Darnley in 1783.

There are two other notable houses in Cobham parish. A little W. of the church is Owletts (NT), a brick mansion from Charles II's reign. This belonged to, and was restored by, Sir Herbert Baker who left it to the National Trust, together with a singularly perfect Yeoman's House at Sole Street, a mile to the S.

COLDRED—*in North Downs, inland from Dover.*
A little village on the edge of Waldershare Park. It sits within a bold defensive rampart which probably marks it as a Saxon burgh. The tiny church is dedicated to a saint popular with the Saxons, St Pancras, and is itself at least partly Saxon.

COLDRUM—see *Trottiscliffe.*

COOLING—*on Hoo peninsula.*
The land rises a little above the flat Thames marshes. The place has enough atmosphere to justify the identification with the opening scene of *Great Expectations* and sure enough here are the graves of Pip's brothers and sisters just outside the South door of the picturesque church—looking as if 'they had all been born on their backs with their hands in their trouser-pockets'. Just around the corner from the church is one of the

Cooling Castle

sights of Kent. During the Hundred Years War French raiders penetrated far up the Thames and Sir John de Cobham, whose brass is seen in Cobham Church, fortified his house to discourage them. This castle, of about 1385, has a spectacular top-heavy gatehouse and elaborate moated defences within. The copper 'charter' on the gate-tower is unique. The history of the castle was uneventful.

COURT-AT-STREET—see *Lympne*.

COWDEN—*Wealden village on Surrey–Sussex borders.*
Kent Ditch (the county boundary) is very near. Cowden had its great days in the age of the iron industry, of which a large

and beautiful furnace pond remains. Crippenden, a house to the N., belonged to the iron-master. There are some lovely houses hereabouts. On the Sussex borders there are pretty woods and commonland.

A very charming village street bends around the churchyard. The church has a high wooden tower and spire appropriate to this forest country.

COXHEATH—see *Linton*.

CRANBROOK—*in centre of the Kentish Weald.*

A little market town which competes with Tenterden for the title of Capital of the Weald. Cranbrook lacks Tenterden's fine High Street and its excellent shops but it has one incomparable possession, the Union Mill. This great smock mill dating from 1814 is in working order and is arguably the finest in the country. It dominates the town from every side.

There is a big school here, founded in Elizabeth's reign. The buildings are a mixed bag, some good, and more indifferent. Not so the church, which is very good indeed. A huge building in golden wealden sandstone, its splendours giving evidence of the town's prosperity in the cloth trade of the 15th and 16th centuries. Monuments to the Roberts family of Glassenbury and others.

The town is full of good things, including much admirable brick and tile-hanging. At the far end of the High Street the new Council Offices are well up to the standard of the old buildings without any phoney antiquarianism.

The area is rich in old buildings, many of them very lovely, and there is an abundance of good walks, especially in Angley Woods and Glassenbury Park.

Cranbrook, Union Mill

CROCKHAM HILL—*on greensand ridge near the Surrey border.*

This is famous for its view of the Weald which is, for some, the noblest as well as the widest prospect in Kent (admittedly it includes much of Surrey and Sussex!) In the immediate foreground is the little church, a neat essay in early Victorian Gothic. It is a place of pilgrimage as the burial place of Octavia Hill, a formidable and very great lady who fought for many good causes and was co-founder of the National Trust. She is buried in the church yard but has an admirable monument in the church.

Appropriately there is National Trust land here, and there are fine walks among the hills.

CRUNDALE—*in North Downs E. of Stour gap.*
A very small scattered village in beautiful downland country. Narrow lanes lead by way of Waltham and Street End to Canterbury. This is essentially walking country, offering tracks by open down and wood to Hastingleigh and Wye. One of the best of these starts at the Norman church which stands all on its own on a high point.

CURTISDEN GREEN—see *Goudhurst.*

DARENT, RIVER—*a stream of Holmesdale.*
The Darent rises near Westerham and flows E. along Holmesdale to Dunton Green where it turns N. to pass through a wide gap in the North Downs. It enters the Thames N. of Dartford (i.e. Darentford). The Darent gap between Otford and Farningham has some of the best scenery in the downs and the river is closely associated with Lullingstone Castle and Roman Villa, Eynsford Castle and St Johns Jerusalem.

DARENTH—*in North Downs S. of Dartford.*
The parish has grown hugely in recent years through the erection of some dreadful housing estates which have been put up with little regard for the character of the landscape. Happily they are hidden from the old village which stands just above the Darent. Here is a church of exceptional interest. Saxon nave and Norman choir, the latter with a low vault (there is an upper storey, now inaccessible). The font is Norman too, covered with splendidly weird sculpture, dragons and the like.

The area was populous in Roman times, and a large villa was discovered near the church.

DARTFORD—*town at crossing of the Darent S. of Thames marshes.*
The town was important in the Middle Ages, with a priory

founded in 1346, and a staging post on Watling Street. A little evidence remains of this past, but the town is crowded, noisy and industrialized. Good local museum near the river. The chief reminder of the coaching days, and perhaps the best thing in the town, is the Bull (later Royal Victoria and Bull) Hotel which still retains its yard intact, although now roofed.

DAVINGTON—see *Faversham*.

DEAL—*seaside town N. of Dover.*
This might be one of the most interesting and attractive of towns, but extensive war-damage—it was within shelling distance of the French coast—decay and confusion have destroyed much and left the promise largely unrealized. Deal was a limb of the Cinque Port of Sandwich and had a lively maritime history. A certain agreeable fishiness lingers on the front N. of the pier; to the S. seedy gentility is to the fore.

This vulnerable coast—Caesar probably landed here in 55 B.C.—was defended during the invasion scare of 1539 by three of Henry VIII's blockhouse castles. Of these Sandown has vanished but for some improbable foundations on the foreshore, Walmer was later altered to provide an official home for the Lord Warden of the Cinque Ports, but Deal Castle is probably the best surviving of all these fortresses of the gunpowder age. It is open regularly (D of E). Walmer Castle is also open, and has relics of famous Lord Wardens including Pitt and Wellington. St George's, in the High Street, is a complete Georgian church, a rarity in Kent; not bad either. An older church, St Leonard's, in Upper Deal, shows a glorious mixture of Norman, Baroque and Victorian in agreeable proportions.

A stroll among the streets of Deal and Walmer will disclose many attractive corners, good houses and odd details among the muddle. Other attractions are the Walmer lifeboat, famous for its work on the Goodwins, the Royal Marine barracks, and the time-ball—alas no longer working—which kept shipping in touch with Greenwich Time.

DENTON—*in North Downs S.E. of Canterbury.*
The little village has too much traffic for its own comfort but it has retained its charm. The country around, especially on the narrow by-roads into the Elham Valley, is exceptionally delightful. This is Ingoldsby country. An old farmhouse in a dell W. of the main road is Tappington, a name familiar to all who read R. H. Barham's dated but still enjoyable masterpiece. The village inn has been renamed the Jackdaw in honour of the Ingoldsby story and has a good sign. Very pretty houses around a tiny square. Church and Court stand together away from the village in a pleasing but undistinguished group.

DETLING—*below North Downs N.E. of Maidstone.*
Well known during the War as a Battle of Britain station, now the setting for the County Agricultural Show. The village is now bypassed and has regained a little of its peace. The Pilgrims Way goes through the village, past the excellent inn (food) and the wall of Court Lodge with its Tudor brick gate. The church is a little below the Way in a pretty setting with fine trees and a great barn. It is part Norman and has a homely broach spire in the Wealden manner. Inside is a major treasure, a superbly carved lectern of the 14th century. Such a splendid piece seems out of place here; no doubt it belonged originally to Boxley Abbey, about three miles away along the valley.

Some agreeable walks start in Detling, some going up into the hills, another following the contour to Boxley Church.

DODDINGTON—*in North Downs midway between Lenham and Faversham.*
Not much shows up on the main road, but just W. is the big park of Doddington Place (gardens sometimes open) and in a corner of this is the church, which looks endearingly comical

from the outside with its white wooden tower. Inside is quite another matter, for here is handsome work of the early 13th century, surprisingly elegant in such a rustic setting. Many good details and fittings.

DODE—*see Birling.*

DOVER—*East Coast port.*
Second to Canterbury as a tourist centre. Its history is continuous from Roman times, and it has been closely associated with national affairs for all these centuries. As the principal Channel Port and the nearest point to the Continent Dover has seen soldiers, statesmen and saints and most of the kings and queens of England.

The town is tightly packed into the narrow valley of the River Dour, producing a slight feeling of claustrophobia but restricting the untidy sprawl which is the fate of most Kent towns. It is not a beautiful town but it is certainly intensely interesting.

Of historic buildings the Castle is the most conspicuous and the most impressive. Supremely well sited on the Eastern Heights it catches the eye from every approach, whether from the sea or from the downland roads. There was a Saxon earthwork here just before the Conquest, and here too is a Saxon church (St Mary's) which is of the greatest importance; ignore, if you can, the awful public-lavatory decor of the Victorian restoration, and concentrate on the fine proportions and the ambitious scale of this pre-Conquest work. Just beside this is a tall tower, the Pharos, which was one of a pair of lighthouses which guided ships into the Roman port (the foundations of its twin exist on the Western Heights). The Norman castle is mostly of Henry II's reign, and the keep is possibly the finest and the best preserved in the country. Note particularly the well and two lovely Norman chapels. What makes Dover

Constable's Gate, Dover Castle

Castle so rarely interesting is that it has been an active fortress for almost the whole of its long life; only recently has the garrison been withdrawn. These walls, towers and underground passages were for use, not for show.

On the opposite hill, the Western Heights, there are other fortifications only less impressive. These date from the invasion scares of the Napoleonic Wars, and are extraordinarily complex, representing a colossal engineering achievement. Not all is accessible, but enough to stagger the visitor and exhaust him physically.

Between these two great defensive structures is the town, which has nothing else as impressive to show except the complicated harbour works. Recent very exciting archaeological discoveries have revealed the history of the Saxon Shore fort of the 3rd century and some of the foundations may be preserved. The civic church, St Mary's, has a grand Norman tower but nothing much else except the municipal trappings. The other Norman church was damaged, together with much else in the town, during the War, and only a few tempting fragments remain. In the heart of the town is the Maison Dieu, now the Town Hall, a big open hall largely of the 14th century which was a pilgrim's hostel; this is nearly very impressive. Next door is a charming Charles II town house (now the Public Library) with a wholly delightful facade. The Benedictines had an important house in Dover, of which some 12th century and later buildings are incorporated in Dover College. There is a neat, recently restored 13th century chapel nearer the centre of the town.

There is good country on either side of the valley. A cliff path goes beyond the castle to St Margaret's and so on to Kingsdown, exploring the least spoilt coastline in Kent. To the W. is the famous headland of Shakespeare's Cliff.

DUNKIRK—*see Hernhill.*

DYMCHURCH—*on the coast of Romney Marsh.*
Dymchurch Wall, towards Hythe, was an important agent in the reclamation of the Marsh, and Dymchurch is, after New Romney and Lydd, the leading parish of Romney Marsh. New Hall, by the church, is the administrative headquarters of the Lords of the Level who run the affairs of the Marsh. With this status and history Dymchurch is disappointing, a village overwhelmed by the weight of day-trippers and holiday-campers. There is a wide windy beach, backed by Martello towers left over from the Napoleonic wars (one is open to the public). Dr Syn's church (visitors will not find that enterprising fictional parson in the records) is tucked away from the village. There is some interesting Norman detail.

EASTCHURCH—*on Sheppey.*
On the island ridge, standing fairly high. There was an air station here (now an open prison) where some pioneering flights were made by Brabazon and others. A monument to these efforts stands by the road. The great house of Sheppey was here, and shabby remains above the village give tantalizing evidence of its former splendours; these are early Tudor work in brick. The church shows signs of its connection with Boxley Abbey, for its grandeur is quite out of proportion to the standing of the village then or now. It is rich work of mid-15th century in a manner which is foreign to Kent; the roof and the screen would be more at home in East Anglia.

A road runs from Eastchurch to the northernmost tip of Sheppey at Warden Point. The old village and its church have long since gone over the crumbing cliffs. Eastwards Sheppey deteriorates into a desert of bungalows and caravans and ends in the bird-haunted emptiness of Shellness.

EASTRY—*W. of Sandwich.*
This is a big village on the road from Sandwich to Dover. It was a royal manor of the Saxon kings and relics crop up from

time to time. Some nice houses, notably The Aumbry (gardens sometimes open) but as a whole the village does not please. The church however is big and impressive, having a Norman tower and 13th century nave. The immediate surroundings of Eastry are a little dull but to the S. there are woodlands through which the Roman road from Richborough to Dover can be traced.

EASTWELL—*below North Downs N.W. of Ashford.*
The great house, home of the Earls of Winchilsea—an 18th century Countess, Anne Finch, was a forerunner of the Romantic poets—has gone and the great park is not what it was. Only the gatehouse, on a corner of the Ashford road, remains of all that grandeur; it is early Victorian pretending to be baroque and doing it rather well. There also remains the lake, an artificial water which was the centrepiece of an 18th century landscape design. This is now reeded up and attracts birds. On the bank stand the pathetic ruins of the parish church which never recovered from war damage and has fallen into decay. Only the tall 15th century tower survives intact. The memorials to past Finches, which made a gallery of monumental sculpture, are now in the Victoria and Albert Museum.

An intriguing legend belongs to Eastwell, of Richard Plantagenet, bastard of Richard III, who is said—and there seems to be something in the tale—to have settled here and to have been buried in the church or churchyard (but surely not in the tomb usually pointed out to visitors).

EBONY—see *Stone-in-Oxney.*

EDEN, RIVER—*Wealden river.*
The Eden rises in Surrey and enters Kent near Edenbridge. At Hever it is widened artificially to form the great lake of Astor's marvellous garden design. It then passes Chiddingstone and enters the Medway just above Penshurst. Not an impressive

stream—although it can be savage in flood—but pleasant and adding agreeably to the charms of the flat Weald.

EDENBRIDGE—*Wealden town on the Surrey border.*
The quiet market town has grown rapidly through the influx of London commuters. Surprisingly not all the growth has been ugly, and new life has been injected into the old. It is now a lively place and begins to promise excellence as a shopping centre. Architecturally there is nothing much here but the big church with its Surrey-like cap to the tower and a few nice houses around the junction of High Street with Church Street. The fine sandstone bridge over the Eden is spoilt by an iron pedestrian bridge alongside.

The best of Edenbridge is its countryside. Lovely country on all sides and especially towards Surrey, where a water mill at Haxton and the Iron Age hillfort of Dry Hill Camp are strong attractions.

EGERTON—*on greensand ridge E. of Maidstone.*
The village is right on the ridge, and the fine church tower is a familiar landmark. Below lies the Weald and the view takes in Tenterden steeple and the Hastings heights. The village is pleasing if without any particular distinction apart from the church. This is a typical Kentish rag building with interesting detail. Note the massive 18th-century candelabrum, and very delightful modern altar rails, their weight carried on the heads of a set of neat saints; you will recognize St James to whom the church is dedicated by the scallop-shell on his mitre.

Lovely houses in the Wealden manner are scattered throughout the parish. It is worth seeking out in particular Link Farm, up a narrow lane ascending the ridge, which is an almost perfect example of the Kentish yeoman's house.

ELHAM—*in North Downs S.E. of Canterbury.*
Elham is the centrepiece of the Elham valley, once almost the most beautiful of Kentish valleys and still, despite the increase

in traffic, and some nasty building, nearly as good as you will find in these parts. In the floor of the valley runs the Nailbourne (or more commonly, in the manner of such streams, it does not flow) and the abandoned track of the old railway from Canterbury to Folkestone. Even if the main road has lost some of its charms the lanes to left and right lead to enchanting country.

Elham has a town-like complexity of small streets which converge on a little square. On one side is a magnificent timber-framed house (now a hotel and restaurant) called the Abbot's Fireside. Massive beams supported by splendidly ugly beasts (or perhaps they are humans). There are good things inside, too. This is the best house, but there are other attractions in brick and tile. Just away from the main road is the church. This has an unobtrusive excellence outside which is no preparation for the riches within. A few recent generations of patrons have filled it with art treasures, woodwork and painting. Far too many to mention here, and visitors must allow plenty of time to enjoy everything. I like especially the reredos in the S. chapel, a 15th century triptych of alabaster panels; the flanking panels show scenes in the life of Becket. On the right he falls under the swords of knights dressed in full plate-armour—a dramatic scene. The celebrated parish library which used to be kept in the parvise of the N. porch is now in Canterbury Cathedral.

EYNSFORD—*in the Darent gap through the North Downs.* In its time this was one of the prettiest villages near London, but commuter pressure and weekend motorists have between them more or less settled its hash. There are still individually good things but the atmosphere has gone.

In the heart of Eynsford there is a ford and a narrow 17th century bridge over the Darent making, with an adjacent black-and-white cottage, a memorable and much photographed scene. Just across the main road from this stands the church which has an unusual—for Kent—tall broach spire. The church is basically Norman, entered through a massive round-headed door and retaining its apse. There has been much complicated later work.

The castle lies between the main road and the river. It is substantially ruined and seems to have been in this state for many centuries. (A nice story has it that William of Eynsford quarrelled with Becket over a matter of patronage—this much is certainly true—and that after the murder and canonization of the Archbishop public opinion turned against William and he abandoned his fortress home. I did not realize that medieval barons were so sensitive!) In its years of ruin Eynsford Castle has been extensively robbed for building stone but, because it has never stood siege or endured 'slighting', the original ground plan is clearer to read than most.

The country around Eynsford is very hilly and, considering the nearness of London, astonishingly unspoilt. There is a good drive up the narrow Knatts Valley and some excellent walks too.

FAIRLAWNE—see *Shipbourne*.

FARNINGHAM—*in Darent Valley*.

Farningham enjoyed the benefit of one of the earliest bypasses and so its charms have escaped close contact with the A20, whose frustrated traffic roars a few hundred yards away. The single village street is pleasing. At the lower end there is a bridge over the Darent providing a view upstream to the mill with its fine millhouse alongside. At the bridge stands a grand coaching inn, as fine an example as one can find in Kent and still dispensing traditional fare. The Lion has its own bridge, too, or so it would seem at a glance, but this is a nice joke because the 'bridge' has height but no breadth.

Although the street is so short there is no sensation of crowding. There is open land beside the admirable modern village hall, and on the opposite side the church is set back behind a generous churchyard. Here is another of the typical Kentish 15th century towers and an excellent example. The curiosity inside is the 15th century font, octagonal and carved with representations of the sacraments of the Church. These Seven Sacrament fonts are a commonplace of East Anglia but rare indeed in the South East. The carving is crude but hearty.

FAVERSHAM—*North of Watling Street.*
A major historic town of Kent, recently rescued from the doldrums and still reviving after its long neglect. Local enterprise directed by knowledge and imagination, and backed astonishingly enough by the borough council as well as by amenity societies and individuals, have wrought something like a miracle here.

Faversham is on a creek running down to the Swale. This gave the place status as a port at an early date, and the history of the town has often been maritime; it had minor standing in the Cinque Ports Federation as a limb of Dover and duly sent its quota of ships to fight the king's enemies, including the Armada. The creek is still there and still operative in a modest way.

An abbey was founded here by King Stephen and he and his consort were buried here. Recent discoveries have shown that this was a very big foundation, and the abbey church was of cathedral proportions. The site is now occupied by the buildings of the new grammar school. A few fragments of the monastic buildings, notably the gate and the chapel-at-the-gate, are built into houses in Abbey Street, but Cromwell's men did an efficient job in destroying so comprehensively a vast complex of buildings.

The parish church stood to the S. of the abbey. It is an odd mixture of a building, thanks mainly to the fall of a central tower. The nave had to be rebuilt in Georgian style and this again was later, and absurdly, translated into neo-Gothic. A new tower and spire were added at the end of the 18th century to give the town its familiar landmark, a tall and elegant lantern which is modelled successfully on Wren's St Dunstan's-in-the-East (itself a variant on the lantern of Newcastle Cathedral). The best of the church is in the choir, where the original stalls survive, complete with poppyheads, arm rests and the best set of misericords in the county. Here is material for an hour of study.

For the rest, central Faversham offers the old grammar school of 1587, a very jolly market hall on stilts, the old gunpowder factory now under restoration, and a walk along Court Street and Abbey Street to see what has been achieved in breathing new life into a fine collection of old houses.

Outside the central area there are two essential visits to make. In Preston, just off Watling Street, there is a church with a remarkable 14th century chancel. The sedilia and piscina are magnificently ornate. At the other end of the town are the buildings of Davington Priory, a nunnery founded in 1153. The monastic buildings are privately owned. The priory church is now the parish church. It is grand late-Norman work, austere but impressive in scale and proportion. A slightly longer journey along Watling Street towards London will take in the lost village of Stone, whose ruined church stands in a cornfield just off the road. Its great interest is that the medieval church incorporated a Roman building, possibly that rarest of relics a Romano-British Christian church.

FOLKESTONE—*on the Channel coast.*

The Kentish watering-place par excellence. Its pre-eminence came late in time, with the railway and with a deliberate policy of development sponsored by Lord Radnor who owned the now-famous Leas. Folkestone has since become synonymous with solid comfort. The Bath-chairs have gone now,

Folkestone Harbour

but retired gentry still enjoy the clean air of the Leas and the more energetic essay the steep paths through the hanging gardens.

That is one kind of Folkestone. There is another in the middle, around the busy harbour, the fish market and the entertainment arcades, and yet another to the E. in the land-slipped tangle of the Warren, still, despite caravans and camping sites, an important nature reserve. The Folkestones are linked by a masterpiece of early Victorian engineering, the superb railway viaduct which sweeps across the little valley which hyphenates the town.

Folkestone had earlier claims to fame. It was a partner in Cinque Ports enterprises as a limb of Dover. It had a Saxon abbey and a Saxon saint, Eanswythe, a Kentish princess, whose bones were—it seems likely—discovered in the 19th century and reburied in the parish church which is dedicated to her. Her shrine and the 12th century work around it are movingly beautiful; the rest of the church is aggressively ornate in the bullying way of the late 19th century.

Behind the town the gault valley ends abruptly and the North Downs sweep upward in almost their most dramatic manner. The backcloth to Folkestone is provided by an irregular ridge, unusually treeless, in the centre of which rises Caesar's Camp, ringed by the rampart of an Iron Age camp and with a Norman motte within—but no connection with Caesar! The view from here embraces the whole of Romney Marsh and the Fire Hills towards Hastings.

FORDWICH—*on the Stour below Canterbury.*
This was the medieval port of Canterbury and a place of note, with a charter and a mayor to go with it from the 12th to the 19th century. Bureaucrats with no sense of history reformed it out of existence in 1883. It retains its Town Hall, small and yet dignified on the tiny quay. The court room is worth seeing.

There are some very charming houses in the village, all worth while if none is outstandingly fine. There is a celebrated inn by the bridge over the Stour, a stream revered by Isaac Walton for its Fordidge trout.

The church, also beside the river, is of exceptional interest, for its antiquity, for its fittings—for it escaped the usual Victorian clear-out—and for an extraordinary and enigmatic Norman tomb chest which still awaits a convincing interpreter.

GADSHILL—see *Higham*.

GILLINGHAM—*the largest of the Medway towns.*
Local government boundaries, at best confusing, are thoroughly bewildering in the Medway towns. The only time that most citizens know whether they live in Gillingham or Chatham is when the rate demand comes.

There is not a lot in Gillingham for the ordinary visitor. Military memories are evoked at Brompton Barracks, the Royal School of Military Engineering, where there is a museum as well as various memorials to past wars and generals. The old centre of Gillingham is towards the river, where the parish church stands well and offers some attractions including 14th century sedilia and Norman font. The appalling residential sprawl E. and S.E. conceals two interesting modern churches at Twydall and Wigmore. Gillingham's most famous landmark for most of this century has now disappeared; this was an extraordinary 'Tower of Babel' just off Watling Street which was the unfinished temple of the Jezreelites, a sect which flourished briefly around the 1880's.

One more curiosity: Grange, eastward along the estuary, was a minor associate of the Cinque Ports as a limb of Hastings. (This was not quite as crazy as it seems; Grange belonged to a knight of Hastings and paid ship service as a manorial duty.) Fragments of the manor-house and its chapel remain.

Godmersham Place

GODMERSHAM—*in the Stour gap through the North Downs.* A very small place but a lovely one. The setting is superb, below a bold chalk dome which sets off the ancient church tower and makes a back-cloth to the park of Godmersham Place. The church is of great antiquarian interest for its Norman tower and vaulted apse. The bearded archbishop sitting within a late Norman arch in low relief is surely Becket and, if so, nearly a contemporary portrait.

During the summer the grounds of Godmersham Place are opened under the National Gardens Scheme. The spirit of Jane Austen presides over this gracious scene. Her brother Edward was adopted by the Knight family of Godmersham and in due course inherited the estate. Jane was often here, living in a setting uncommonly like that of her novels. The splendid early 18th century house stands on flat ground towards the river, and behind it wooded glades, the central one terminating in a classical temple, rise gently towards the Downs. An exquisite example of 18th century good taste.

The Pilgrims Way passes along the top of the Downs beyond the park.

GOUDHURST—*in the centre of the high Weald.*
The little town sits on a hill which rises to 406 ft; not very high but enough to make it a landmark in the rolling countryside. The church tower, on the actual crown of the hill, commands a magnificent view; if the tower is locked, the view from the edge of the new burial-ground to the S. is some compensation. Goudhurst is full of very attractive houses, which match one another more than is common in Kent, presumably because they were built (or refaced) when, in the 16th century, the cloth trade and the iron industry brought prosperity to the ancient forest settlement. They climb the little hill in a charmingly irregular double line, achieving the kind of harmony which modern planners strive after, often in vain.

The church looks old at first because the squat tower—scene of the poet Richard Church's wartime fire-watching!—is not medieval but Charles I and half classical. The church beyond is 13th and 14th century. The monuments are what catch the eye. Goudhurst was a home of the ubiquitous Culpeper (or Colepeper) family who here lived at Bedgebury, below the hill. Several of the family are commemorated in the church, notably Sir Alexander, who occupies an alcove lit by an oriel window. He and his lady, who lived in Henry VIII's reign, are shown in portrait effigies of painted wood.

There are many good houses in the neighbourhood, including Finchcocks, down in the valley of the Teise, which can be seen from a public footpath; it is a large and imposing mansion of early Georgian times, perhaps too town-like for this gentle countryside. Beyond Bedgebury Park, a high eccentric house complete with spire (it is now a school), are the wide acres of Bedgebury Pinetum. This is nine-tenths laboratory, one-tenth museum and all of it beautiful; run jointly by Kew Gardens and the Forestry Commission to raise and demonstrate coniferous trees. Much of the area is given over to the forest plots, but nearest the road and the car park is a finely landscaped pinetum which take advantage of the rise and fall of the land and of the tiny streams which flow down to Marshall's Lake.

Goudhurst is a hunting-ground for those who like to explore lost railways, for the old branch line from Paddock Wood to Hawkhurst passes below the hill and across the remarkably empty country S.W. of Cranbrook. Another exploration, this time scenic and literary, is to Winchet Hill and Curtisden Green, to the N. Here, superbly placed on top of a Wealden hill, is Bethany School which was founded by an eccentric evangelical preacher in the 19th century. The founder's grandson Frank Kendon, who was born here, recaptured the essence of Kentish life in a memorable autobiography *The Small Years*. Just across the road from Bethany is the converted oast which was long the home of the Kentish poet and novelist Richard Church.

GRAIN—*at confluence of Medway and Thames.*
Still an island by virtue of the Yantlet Channel which joins the two rivers. The old village is still more insulated from the mainland by the huge oil refinery. This may look forbidding, but as usual with these installations the functional structures are surprisingly good to look at. After this the old church, whose tower fails to rise above roof level, is an anticlimax. There are Norman and later details. Beyond, Kent comes to an end in a fascinating wilderness of bramble and concrete

coastal defences.

The village pub, the Cat and Cracker, puns on technicalities of the refinery business.

GRAVESEND—*on Thameside.*
Gravesend's history is tied up with the river. Even today, when its standing as the lowest crossing of the river has been destroyed by the Dartford Tunnel which led to the closing of the car-ferry, it is still involved with the waterside; here ships take on pilots for the navigation of the estuary and Channel.

Apart from the traffic of the river, which may be watched from riverside gardens, there is not much in Gravesend to attract the casual visitor. The town was largely burnt out early in the 18th century, but the resultant Georgian town—which might have been of the greatest interest—was itself largely rebuilt in Victorian times. Admirers of Victoriana ecclesiastical and domestic will find a few interesting things down by the pier and around the clock tower.

The two heroes of Gravesend are Pocahontas and General Gordon. Pocahontas, the Indian girl from Virginia, came to England to be feted at James I's Court and inevitably succumbed to the climate and the diseases of civilization. On her way home she got as far as Gravesend and there died. The church where she was buried was destroyed in the fire, but its replacement is an object of American pilgrimage. Gordon's involvement in Gravesend was more considerable. He was here in charge of defensive works along the Thames and did valiant work for the local poor. Two new schools commemorate him.

GREAT CHART—*in upper Stour valley S.W. of Ashford.*
The village is stretched out along the road from Ashford to Tenterden. It stands at the gates of Godinton Park and the harmony among the Victorian cottages comes from the patronage of the great house. The street rises steadily with

Groombridge

the church right at the top. It is a handsome building set off by a pretty miniature cottage—the so-called Pest House—in front. The best is a 15th century rebuilding of the S. chapel. There are brass memorials to various Tokes of Godinton.

The immediate countryside is not especially attractive but there are several fine houses, notably Yardhurst which lies towards Bethersden.

GROOMBRIDGE—*on Sussex boundary W. of Tunbridge Wells.*

Very small but very perfect; my favourite Kentish village. Just a triangular green tilted sharply with cottages on two sides, the church and park on the third. Just beyond is Kent Ditch and then you are in Sussex. A footpath just beside the churchyard leads through the park and across the head of an ornamental water, then twists to give glimpses of Groombridge Place. If the gardens are open, you will be able to see it even better. Here surely is the loveliest house in Kent. It was built around the time of the Restoration on the site of an older moated house, and, appropriately in this position, it reconciles the older fashions and the new. Rich but by no means gaudy. The gardens are nicely formal.

The Packers who owned Groombridge were Royalists, patriots and Protestants. A Packer of James I's reign viewed with horror the proposed marriage of Charles, Prince of Wales, with the Infanta of Spain. When Charles came home without his bride he joyfully built a chapel by the roadside to commemorate this escape from disaster. The chapel is a nice essay in mock Gothic, rather like the chapel of a minor Oxford college. Very pleasing and atmospheric.

The lane rising from the green towards Ashurst is worth following, partly for several good cottages and a mixed-styled Court Lodge, partly for some superb views over the wooded border country.

HADLOW—*in Medway plain N.E. of Tonbridge.*

Here is the best of Kentish follies. Walter May added a tower to his 'castle' around 1840. It was very tall and slim, 'Gothick' of course, and clearly inspired by Fonthill Abbey. When the castle was demolished not long ago this agreeable absurdity was spared to provide for another century a splendid exclamation mark in this flat country.

Hadlow is the centre of agricultural education in Kent. The new buildings of Hadlow College cover a large area but are pleasingly unobtrusive. There are some big glasshouses, and others nearby, under commercial control, are fantastically huge.

The village has no great attractions and has grown a little too rapidly. There is a pretty corner by the church, whose low conical tower makes a good foil for the castle.

HARBLEDOWN—*on Watling Street just outside Canterbury.* The past and present of this little village are bound up with Canterbury. It is probably Chaucer's 'Bob-Up-and-Down', which is a fair description of the present road. The village is in two bits, of which the West is detached and of no particular interest. The eastern half, which is joined up to Canterbury, is of the greatest interest. The road is winding and very narrow and there is nowhere to leave a car, but it is not too far to walk back from the outskirts of the city. Here the Norman Archbishop Lanfranc established a hospital for 'lepers', that is for infectious diseases. A pretty group of buildings, now almshouses, stands high above the road. They are nearly all Victorian and picturesque. Visitors are welcomed and will be shown various treasures of curiosity value and a set of wooden mazers (14th century or later) which are splendid. The chapel survives from Norman times if not from the foundation, a fine building with some fascinating details.

If this were not enough Harbledown has a medieval parish church as well, just across the road. Nothing much here, but it contributes to a pretty group best seen from a point W. along the road beside a fine old barn.

Harbledown once had a viewpoint towards the city—Golden Hill—which the National Trust owns; unfortunately recent house-building has ruined the prospect. Just beyond Golden Hill the Pilgrims Way traverses its last mile to Canterbury; in the other direction it leads through a pretty sunken way to the heights of Bigbury, the Belgic hillfort which was perhaps the tribal capital or meeting-place before the city was founded in the valley.

HARDRES, UPPER AND LOWER—*small villages in downland east of Stone Street, S. of Canterbury.*
This is lightly populated country traversed by narrow winding roads. Lower Hardres (pronounced Hards) has a plain little

pre-Victorian church and a nice pub (food). Upper Hardres is a scattered village of which the most memorable feature is the huge barn* beside the church. The church, dwarfed and outclassed, has nevertheless a claim to fame, a notable bracket-brass to a parish priest of Henry IV's reign. There are some baroque and classical monuments. Good early glass too.

HARRIETSHAM—*in gault valley below North Downs E. of Maidstone.*

Harrietsham has suffered hideously from motor traffic. The modern road cuts the village neatly into two and, in the present state of traffic, never the twain shall meet. The southern half is grouped around a strip of green with an inn and one or two handsome houses on one side, on the other a fine almshouse range of 1770, the whole making a most charming sight. The little River Len is nearby, offering a nice wet walk downstream to Broomfield. Across the main road is a workaday village street, and quite away from both halves stands the noble church, superbly framed in trees. This has a grand Kentish rag tower and another—and earlier—stunted tower to the N., an intriguing oddity. The font is Norman and very fine indeed.

The Marley tile factory spreads to the E. Westwards there is a pretty walk through to Hollingbourne, and to the N. the hill rises steeply to the lovely beechwoods of Stede Hill, where a Georgian-faced house looks down upon the Pilgrims Way. Beautiful country this and not to be hurried over.

HARTLIP—*in orchard country S. of Watling Street beyond Rainham.*

Terribly near the urban masses of the Medway towns, but Hartlip still survives miraculously. There has been building, much of it very superior in price and style (but mostly traditional). Hartlip shares with Newington and Teynham fame

* *Destroyed by fire in 1972*

for its beauty in cherry-blossom time; then the orchards are from another world. The church is much restored. It still has one of the famous North Kent angle piscinas, and a good one, and also a curiosity in the lean-to cell attached to the tower, probably the home of a holy and unwashed hermit who had dropped out of medieval society.

HARTY—*on Swale shore of Sheppey.*
Harty is one of the islands which make up Sheppey. From the central island road a narrow lane zigzags to the coast, crossing the insulating channel and coming at last to a farm, a pub and a church. This is Harty, one of the lonely places of Kent. Long may it escape the threatened marina and other horrors of civilization. The pub stands at the head of Harty Ferry, where a boat once plied to the mainland near Faversham. This is a place for birds and a memorable sight in the season. You approach the church through the farmyard. It looks as un-

Chest, Harty Church

assuming as a barn but is full of interest. Notice the remains of the rood screen, Royal Arms of George III and—a real treasure —a superb 14th-century chest with a lively carving of a joust on the face, precisely done and yet full of action.

HAWKHURST—*on Sussex border in the Weald.*
Almost a town, or rather a little town and a detached village. The town is laid out on top of the ridge at Highgate around cross-roads. Here is an inn, a row of shops, a Victorian Gothic church and—the best-looking building—almshouses built in 1723. Below the hill on the Sussex side is the Moor, a village green by no means as wild as the name suggests. Here a pretty group of houses is backed by the sandstone church. This was severely damaged in the War and has been well restored, so that it will pass for a typical 13th–14th-century Wealden church, gracious and well-proportioned.

HEADCORN—*centrally in the Weald.*
The main line has brought a fair rash of commuter housing to the old village, but the two mix better than most. The main street is nearly all old and sufficiently varied, not to say muddled, to retain interest. Here is a modest marketing centre for the surrounding area and a place to eat in. At the hub, where the road turns abruptly, there are some grand half-timbered houses, the one on the corner being a cloth hall. There is another good house of the same style behind the church. All these are evidence of a boom in Headcorn during the heyday of Kentish broadcloth. At the far end of the street a reminder of the succeeding age in a toll-house. The big church, late 14th century, is doubtless another product of the age of wool and an impressive one. The River Beult flows through the meadows to the S. and the lane to Frittenden crosses it by a handsome medieval stone bridge.

HEMSTED FOREST—see *Benenden.*

HERNE BAY—*on N. Kent coast.*

Herne Bay has grown with the influx of commuters but has not lost its individual character which is that of an early Victorian seaside resort. It was indeed a 'planted' town of the 1830's and, even though the original scheme was never completed, there is much to amuse and even to charm in the area around an absurd clock-tower on the promenade. But the pier, which was Herne Bay's special pride, is in a sad state. The sea front is very long and offers at least a bracing walk. At the far western end there is a view across the bay towards Swalecliffe which looks very well at sunset; at the eastern end the Downs rise mildly above the sea, with a gentle stroll along the top all the way to Reculver.

The original village of Herne is a mile or so inland beyond Thanet Way. A landmark on the way is Herne Mill, one of the last windmills in Kent to fall out of use and now almost swallowed up in new houses. The centre of Herne is not spoilt. A double kink in the Canterbury road gives it the required enclosed look and the old houses and inn are set off by a very fine church. The brasses and monuments are worth study but nothing is so good as the rich and massive tower. The building is largely of a piece and that belonging to the 14th century. Ridley, the martyred Bishop of Oxford, was rector here when he had as neighbour at Ford Palace Archbishop Cranmer who later followed him to the stake.

HERNHILL—*in wooded country above the Thames estuary N. of Watling Street.*

This is in the Blean and there are still plenty of woods around, some of them offering good walking. The parish is scattered but the village proper is almost as pretty as Kent can offer. The village green is set around with church, inn, pretty cottages and the manor-house. What more could you ask? The church is singularly perfect in its unfussy

15th century manner. The cottages are Victorian rustic-domestic at its most discreet. The Red Lion is an old yeoman's house.

In Hernhill churchyard are buried the pathetic victims of the Battle of Bossenden Wood, when in 1838 a deranged 'Messiah' led a gang of depressed farm labourers against the militia. The whole story, much more incredible than any fiction, is told in *Battle in Bossenden Wood* by P. G. Rogers, 1961. As a direct result the church and school were built on Dunkirk Hill to improve the moral and intellectual stability of the rural population!

HEVER—*Wealden village near Surrey border.*
Henry VIII dominates the village from the inn sign and he is certainly type-cast for the role of ogre in the local legends. Hever was a manor of the Boleyn family and Anne spent much of her early life in the little moated and fortified house to which the slightly misleading title of 'castle' is given. It was the scene of much of the prolonged royal courtship which triggered off a social, economic and religious revolution. Like the home of Anne Boleyn's old friend Thomas Wyatt at Allington, Hever fell on bad times in the Victorian age, and it was largely derelict when William Waldorf Astor acquired it and set about transforming the house and its setting. The little Tudor brick 'village' beyond the moat is his work and so is the superb Italian garden, enriched with art treasures brought back from his travels, with the great lake beyond which was formed out of the little River Eden. If there is more new than old to be seen now, the new work is extremely well done, expert craftsmanship being matched with scholarship. A visit is a rewarding experience.

The village is charming, clustered around the castle gates in feudal style. In the middle is the church with a tall spire. The best thing here—and it is very good—is the memorial brass of

Sir Thomas Boleyn, Anne's ambitious and ruthless father. Not the nicest of characters, but he is commemorated with one of the very last great brasses in England, a fine combination of formality and portraiture.

There are some most agreeable walks in the soft wooded country around Hever.

HIGHAM—*in North Downs W. of Medway towns.*
The village sign at Gadshill commemorates Dickens and rightly, for he is the greatest 'lion' of Higham. Another is Falstaff, who ambushed the travellers here and is remembered in a pub on the old highway. Opposite this is Gadshill Place, now a school, a modest house of about 1780 which Dickens coveted for much of his life and which became his last home. He wrote in a chalet (now in the grounds of Eastgate Museum, Rochester) which stood in a little garden across the road and which was approached by tunnel. Here he wrote the last completed pages of his unfinished novel of Rochester *The Mystery of Edwin Drood* on the last day of his life. Another local worthy who campaigned for the Reform Act of 1832 is remembered by an obelisk on the high point of the village.

Higham itself is large and shapeless, almost defying anyone to identify its shape and anatomy. The old heart is away to the N., on the edge of the marshes, where there was a small Benedictine priory, now vanished. Near the site is the parish church, now almost literally the last building in the parish. It has considerable charm as well as antiquarian interest. Striped with flints like a humbug, it is a muddly building but the excellent fittings, including an almost complete rood screen, make up for deficiencies in plan. Beyond, the flats lead to infinity, making the churchyard one of many claimants to be the original of Pip's churchyard in *Great Expectations.*

HIGH HALDEN—*in the high Weald N.W. of Tenterden.*
The new village spreads along the Ashford road but the old is

concentrated neatly around a green. Beyond is pleasing rolling country in which Tenterden's St Michael's spire is a feature. The Chequers occupies one side of the square, a solid and good-looking inn about which a book *The Chequers Inn* by L. W. Martin has been written. It looks over to the slim shingled spire of the church which is of a kind rarely seen in this forest country although it would look at home in Essex. The weight of the belfry is borne on a criss-crossed structure of massive timbers, a most impressive example of rustic engineering.

HIGH HALSTOW—*in Hoo peninsula.*

This is relatively high (about 150 ft) and to the north the land drops quickly to the Thames marshes, evoking memories of Dickens' terrifying and benevolent convict. Indeed High Halstow is one of the many candidates for fame as the original of Pip's village in *Great Expectations.* The old forge stands across from the church, a timber-framed house. A wooded hill to the N., blocking the view of the marshes, is a RSPB reserve incorporating a heronry (admission by permit) and the neighbourhood is astonishingly rich in wild life and indeed in rural charms. The church is bulky and impressive, showing 15th century additions to a largely 13th century building.

HINXHILL—*in gault valley E. of Ashford.*

So discreet that most travellers pass by without realizing the existence of this tiny village. Just a farm, a large and rather aggressively white mansion, and a church looking across to Wye Down. Early spring is the time to come here when the churchyard is completely carpeted with snowdrops and lambs are in the fields. The church is of minor interest, but the setting is the thing. Peace and quiet, so elusive in the South-East, are here.

HOLLINGBOURNE—*in gault valley N.E. of Maidstone.*
The main A20 happily misses the village, although too many large vehicles take the steep downland road to Sittingbourne. There is a long village, almost two in fact. Nearest the main road is Eyhorne Street, which has recently lost a great Georgian mansion by neglect and destruction, and now makes do with a delectable collection of cottages and inns. Then comes a gap, with some new housing and one gorgeous Elizabethan black-and-white house, and fields and trees make an appropriate foreground to the upper village. Here are the church and the manor-house. This is Culpeper country and the great family have their own 17th century N. chapel with monuments (including a beautiful effigy of Elizabeth Culpeper who was the first to lie in the new chapel). The family lived at Greenway to the E., but this is now much decayed and the great house is Hollingbourne Manor, just N. of the church. This is a very big house, in mellow Elizabethan brick with a fine wall to the road. One of the most exciting and satisfying Tudor buildings in Kent.

The upper village is set beautifully against the swell of the Downs. The Pilgrims Way passes just N. of the inn and here becomes a bridle way as far as Harrietsham. Much lovely downland country to the N.

HOLMESDALE—*the narrow clay valley between North Downs and greensand ridge.*
The name is usually applied to the western valley from Sevenoaks to the Surrey border and beyond, but it might equally be used for the eastern continuation to Folkestone. One of the most characteristic features of Kentish landscape, and one which is equally beautiful and historic.

The modern roads A25, M20 and A20 follow the valley pretty closely.

HOO ST WERBURGH—*on Hoo peninsula and Medway estuary.*

The once lonely village which Dickens knew is by no means lonely now. It continues to grow, the normal high rate of the South-East accelerated by the influence of the oil refinery at Grain and the power-station at Kingsnorth. Under these pressures much that was charming has vanished. In a corner by the church the Dickensian atmosphere survives precariously. The church is very nearly very good, an earlier building transformed in the 15th century. The roof is unusual for Kent, an attempt to do with inadequate skill what the master carpenters of East Anglia were doing for their great churches. Well worth seeing.

The fascinating marshes have almost been lost now. There is a walk through to Upnor (reached by road via Frinsbury) which is the most interesting settlement of the estuary. A hamlet which turns its back on the land and serves the water. Now much frequented by sailing folk. The tall ship is *T.S. Arethusa*, a floating school for, mainly, the Merchant Navy. A little to the S. is Upnor Castle, a blockhouse built in Elizabeth's reign as part of the defensive system for the naval base at Chatham. It failed dismally to do just this a century later when the Dutch fleet sailed by, and some of the present buildings were put up—stable-door fashion—afterwards.

HORSMONDEN—*in the high Weald.*

The village is set around a large green. The new housing estates are placed discreetly out of sight, and all is, if quite undistinguished, quietly satisfactory. So much for the main village. But Horsmonden hides its principal charms. The old village is a mile and more away among the tangle of narrow lanes which twine around Rectory Park, where the Smith-Marriotts, rectors and lords of the manor, lived. This is civilized parkland yielding views across to Goudhurst on its hill.

Looking over to its neighbour Horsmonden church stands well on high ground, alone except for a cottage and farm buildings. The tower is of mellow wealden sandstone which makes it look as if it grew out of the soil. Inside are memorials to Austens of Broadford, ancestors of the immortal Jane.

The Austens were in the cloth trade. The other industry of these parts was iron. The Gun, a pub on the green, reminds us of an important product of the furnace which operated a half-mile away. Everything has gone now except the furnace pond, a wide and beautiful stretch of water which once provided power for the great bellows of the blast furnace.

HOTHFIELD—*in sandy country between Ashford and Charing.* The A20 cuts across Hothfield Common, a nature reserve which provides a home for plants and insects. Sometimes a nature trail is laid out to show the most interesting features. The village lies beyond the common where it serves as an open green. There is no great interest here. Just beyond, a long wall once protected the home of the Earls of Thanet. Now the Earls have gone, leaving only the timber of the great park to testify to past grandeur. There is also the church, tucked away within the park wall, with its noble monument to Sir John Tufton who lived in James I's reign. He restored the church after a disastrous fire.

This valley of the Great Stour is one of great houses. Godinton, to the E., has lasted better than Hothfield Place. It is a pretty gabled mansion, also of James I, set in a big park. If you enter—and the house is opened with generous frequency—you will find that the brick frame masks an older house with great hall. Upstairs there is some fascinating 17th century detail, notably a shallow relief showing the Kentish militia in training. In a corner of the park is Swinford Old Manor, now a school, where the poet laureate Alfred Austin played the rural squire.

Furnace Pond, Horsmonden

HUNTON—*in the valley of the Beult.*
The flat country just at the foot of the greensand escarpment is not immediately appealing but it becomes very important to those who yield to its quiet charms. Two principal pockets of population are separated by the wide park of Hunton Court, where Campbell-Bannerman, briefly Prime Minister, lived. The house is plain, the gardens—opened from time to time—pleasing, the park magnificent. Close to the mansion is the church, its 13th century tower capped with a blunt spire. There are monuments to Fanes and some elegant medieval details.

The area is rich in small houses of quality as well as some handsome oasts, mostly now turned into delectable houses. The river is very pretty and it can be followed by footpath for a mile or two upstream.

HYTHE—*set back from the sea to the W. of Folkestone.*
This was one of the original Cinque Ports, a major port in the days when the River Rother reached the sea here. But the river shifted westwards and shingle built up to block the harbour. Now the sea is half a mile away with a row of Victorian houses on the front. The medieval town is high and dry. A High Street, full of pubs and traffic, offers no great attractions, but beyond and above it steep streets climb the old cliffs, giving fine views out to sea. Here are some charming houses, a few of medieval origin but mostly dating from the town's 18th century revival. The precipitous Church Hill, closed to traffic, is full of good things.

Here too is St Leonard's the only survivor of Hythe's four ancient churches. This, for once, is not a building of modest charm but a major masterpiece. The church was enlarged in the 13th century, when by a happy coincidence the prosperity of the port and the Early English style were both at their height. Because of the very steep and confined site the new

Wealden Meadow, Hunton

work had to be raised up above a processional passage; this meant that the choir, like that of Canterbury Cathedral, rose above the nave by a flight of steps. The effect is most dramatic. The chancel arch and the tall piers of the choir are plain and majestic. Underneath the choir, and alas! attracting far more attention than the architecture, is the so-called crypt, the enclosed processional way, which is crammed with bones, presumably the scourings of the restricted graveyard over many centuries. Forget any stories about Saxon battles and Danish raiders!

IDE HILL—*on greensand ridge S.W. of Sevenoaks.*
Ide Hill, distinguished from its neighbours by the slim spire of a Victorian church, is the centrepiece of the hills which look across the Weald and into Sussex. There is a string of National Trust properties along the ridge, at Toys Hill, Chartwell and Mariners Hill, all with fine prospects. Perhaps the best view is from Ide Hill, not from the National Trust land itself, which is wooded, but from the car-park below, from which the land drops away in a semicircular amphitheatre. Below the hill glistens the new Bough Beech reservoir, haunt of many birds, and the backcloth of the view is Ashdown Forest rising to a dome at Crowborough Beacon.

The village is a 19th century development with many pretty, undistinguished houses. Emmets, on the road to Sundridge, belongs to the National Trust and has a garden which is shown regularly.

Ide Hill makes a base for some of the best walks in West Kent.

IGHTHAM—*in greensand country E. of Sevenoaks.*
The busy A25 now bypasses the village, for which relief much thanks. There is a stylish square formed by a slight widening of the road, and here is a half-timbered inn and some attractive cottages. The Town House (meals) on the corner is more

notable. The church is detached to the N. and now overlooks the bypass. It is a homely building with monuments to the Selbys, including Dame Dorothy Selby who is associated, by some confusion of evidence, with the revelation of the Gunpowder Plot. She has a portrait monument with a memorable if enigmatic epitaph.

The Selbys lived at Ightham Mote, which is two miles to the S. along a byroad through Ivy Hatch. Approached from this side you get an almost aerial view descending the steep greensand hill. There is hardly a better sight in West Kent. This is an early 14th century house, added to through the centuries without spoiling the general effect, standing wholly within a rectangular moat. The house is open once a week and visitors may admire the hall and chapel and the many lovely details. If unluckily you arrive on the wrong day, a fair view of the exterior may be had from the public path which skirts the S. side of the moat.

Ightham Mote is in the heart of fine country. A footpath through the farmyard opposite the Mote climbs up to One Tree Hill (National Trust) which gives superb views over the Weald and the return may be made through the birchwoods N. of the escarpment. There is further N.T. land at Oldbury Hill, W. of the village and just off the A25. This steep round hill, overgrown with silver birch, records two stages of prehistory. On the N.E. face, just beyond an ancient sunken road which bisects the hill, there are shallow caves in the rock which were the homes of people of the Old Stone Age—and very uncomfortable they must have been. The hill is surrounded by the rampart and ditch of an Iron Age hillfort. Oldbury gives good views to the E. and the scene is especially beautiful in autumn.

IVYCHURCH—*on Romney Marsh.*
In this flat country, the tiny village is marked by a group of

trees, making it look like an island in the green sea. Inn, church and a clutch of cottages huddle companionably together. The church is most impressive, possibly the finest on the Marsh. Its ragstone walls and tower are beautifully weathered and glow a pale gold in sunlight. The S. porch is tall and almost throws the whole design out of scale. Inside the church seems even vaster than out; it is a huge open and almost empty hall. What a setting for drama and music it would make, and what a subject for a painter of the Flemish School!

KEMSING—*in Holmesdale, just below the North Downs to the N.E. of Sevenoaks.*

The railway station was placed, by a singular official perversity, more than a mile outside the village, but Kemsing has nevertheless become a commuter village with extensive new housing almost linking it with Otford to the W. The old village has been left largely untouched. Here is a little enclosed green in which rises St Edith's Well, a natural spring associated with a saintly Saxon princess. Brick and tile cottages surround it. It is all quietly civilized, the kind of scene which Randolph Caldecott, who lived here, liked to paint. To the N., between the village street and the Pilgrims' Way, is the church which may have Saxon origins but whose present appearance is late Victorian and Edwardian. It presents an incredible display of dark and heavily dated art. Individually the pieces are often good but no one knew when to stop. In the churchyard there is a jolly wavy crinkle-crankle wall.

A number of tracks climb up to the Downs, leading to some delightful and unspoiled country. Along the Pilgrims' Way to the E. there is a view of St Clere, an enormous mansion which seems to date from the 1630's and is a pioneer of the 'new' architecture of the Restoration. Just beyond, the Way becomes, for the first time in Kent, an unmetalled track through the fields.

KINGSDOWN—*in North Downs above Wrotham Hill.*
There are several Kingsdowns in Kent, but only one—West Kingsdown—is of particular note. First impressions here are disastrous. The main A20 is littered with shabby bungalows and petrol stations, and beyond this all principles of planning seem to have been abandoned. To the N.W. there is the roar of Brands Hatch, to the S.E. only a smock mill to please the eye briefly.

This, happily, is a false view of Kingsdown. Across the main road to the W. narrow lanes lead through woods and open valleys to some of the highest and loneliest country near London. On the other side, insulated from the housing estates by a little wood, is the parish church, a Saxon foundation with what may have been one of the tower-naves of the late Saxon period. The church was remodelled in Norman times and there are fragments of contemporary wall-paintings in the deep window recesses. It is an appealing and evocative building in its precarious loneliness.

KINGSGATE—see *Broadstairs.*

KITS COTY—see *Aylesford.*

KNOLE—see *Sevenoaks.*

KNOWLTON—*in downland S.W. of Sandwich.*
There is no village, only the Court, the Dower House and the church at the end of a long drive. Knowlton Court is an Elizabethan house, much changed. The Dower House, whose charming garden may be visited once or twice a year, is newer by half a century or so and closer to its original state. The church is mostly a Victorian rebuilding but the monuments to Peytons and Narboroughs who lived here have been retained. The group of buildings is pleasantly isolated from the workaday world.

Knowlton has a small part in the romantic story of Dorothy

Osborne and William Temple who were devoted and frustrated lovers during the Commonwealth. Some of Dorothy's exquisite letters were written from Knowlton where she was staying with Sir Thomas Peyton, her brother-in-law.

LAMBERHURST—*Wealden village on Sussex border.*
On this side of the county Kent ends magnificently with some of its very best scenery. Lamberhurst village itself is difficult to evaluate because the main road traffic on the A21 pounds through its heart ceaselessly; it was even worse before the little bridge over the Teise was widened. There are no exceptional buildings in the street, but the brick and tile are pleasing. The big house, Court Lodge, square Georgian and surrounded by a charming garden, is tucked away above the village beside the handsome spired church. The church fittings are interesting; they include a Jacobean pulpit and elegant Royal Arms of Queen Anne. The churchyard overlooks the lush Teise valley, in which an enjoyable footpath walk leads down to Goudhurst.

Lamberhurst was a major centre of the iron industry, which in part accounts for the air of prosperity and the town-like appearance which it wears. The forge was in the Teise Valley nearer the Sussex border, and here were cast the famous iron railings which stood around St Paul's Cathedral. Just above the forge the Teise flows through the park of Bayham Abbey, which here forms the county boundary. Lord Camden's great Victorian quasi-Jacobean mansion stands high above the Kent bank but the beautiful remains of the Praemonstratensian Abbey of Bayham, founded in Richard I's reign, are just in Sussex. A pity! We just fail to possess the finest monastic ruin in the South-East (now in public care and opened regularly).

Bayham is picturesque mainly because of the operation of Time, a little assisted during the 18th century Gothic revival.

Bayham Abbey, Lamberhurst

Scotney, to the S.E., is calculatedly picturesque, an outstanding masterpiece of the 19th century passion for landscape design. The original castle was medieval, a little moated and fortified manor-house of Richard II's reign. Originally it had four top-heavy corner towers. Three of these have gone leaving a sole survivor which is endearingly comical rather than impressive. On the site two houses were built, one tile-hung and homely, the other elegant and stylist. In the 1830's Edward Hussey built a new 'castle' on the hill above the damp old site, landscaped the steep hill and the quarry from which stone for the new house came, and then partly demolished the old buildings to give them the appropriately delapidated picturesqueness. This enchanting essay in landscape design was given by the descendant of the original deviser to the National Trust and it may be visited regularly. At its best in autumn.

LEEDS—*in sandy country in Len Valley E. of Maidstone.*
The village lies S. of the A20 and has some charm, with a number of attractive houses. Notice particularly, on a back lane behind the church, Battel Hall, a stone hall-house of the 14th century. The church has an incredibly solid Norman tower, and much of the original rood screen survives. There was a priory at Leeds too, but this has gone literally without trace.

Leeds is famous for its castle (strictly speaking in the neighbouring parish of Broomfield). There is a magnificent park, landscaped in the 18th century, through which the little River Len trickles. The castle is moated by a lake on which the buildings seem to float. (They can be seen from the main road, a footpath crosses the park, and the grounds are sometimes opened under the National Gardens Scheme.) The scene is unbelievably picturesque, and incredulity is in order for all is not what it seems. The medieval castle, by custom a possession of the King's Consort, has acquired 1820ish neighbours

Leeds Castle

which match, enthusiastically but unconvincingly, its turrets and battlements.

LEIGH—*in low Weald W. of Tonbridge.*
Pronounced Lye. Passing through in a hurry one gets a fleeting impression of a model Tudor village, all timber-framing and red brick. Stop and look and the truth quickly becomes plain. This is a very pretty phony, put up in Victorian times, much of it at the same time as Hall Place, the big house which lies behind the high brick wall lining the village street. Even parts of the church are of the same date. It is all highly pleasing, especially seen at the discreet distance of the green on a hot summer day with cricketers exerting themselves in the foreground. The gardens of Hall Place are frequently opened and reward the visitor; they give a close view of the Victorian Tudor house of the 1870's.

Leigh stands a little above the valley of the Medway, here a small pretty stream reached by minor road or on foot by a track behind the green which goes towards Tonbridge through charming scenery. There is a still better walk through Penshurst Park which culminates in a fine view of the Place.

LEN, RIVER—*a stream of the greensand country.*
The little Len rises between Lenham and Harrietsham and flows through Leeds Castle park and Mote Park to meet the Medway just below the Archbishop's Palace. This mild stream was an important factor in industry, providing the power for flour, paper and fulling mills. It also contributed to several major landscaping scenes. It still has some pretty corners, in Leeds Park, at the big mill pond behind the Great Danes Hotel and of course in Mote Park.

LENHAM—*a small town of the Gault Valley midway between Maidstone and Ashford.*
The A20 just misses Lenham and so it escapes the worst of the

traffic; it has also escaped the more insidious blight of the 'beauty spot'. Although it is potentially almost as attractive as Chilham it is still unselfconscious. Long may it stay that way.

The centrepiece of Lenham is the Square, which has a rather messy building in the middle but very agreeable houses, now mostly pubs or shops, around. In one corner an ancient lych-gate leads into the churchyard. On the right, over the wall, a magnificent barn may be seen. The church itself is townlike in scale and most handsome, especially in its fittings. Note the stone altar slab, also choir stalls, pre-Reformation lectern, and a most notable pulpit, Jacobean or earlier.

The best house is just up the Headcorn road, a compact, slightly top-heavy town-house bearing the date 1621.

Although Lenham seems to lie low it is in fact on the watershed. The Great Stour rises in a farm just to the E., the Len a little farther to the W. The Downs are very near to the N., a conspicuous slope displaying one of the two chalk war-memorial crosses of Kent. This is just above the Pilgrims Way, here a particularly lovely field-path. Good walking country here. The lanes to the S. are better for leisured motoring.

LEYBOURNE—*in Holmesdale N.W. of Maidstone.*
A main-road village now which has lost much of its charm. There is really nothing left to note but the little group around the church, but there are good things here. Leybourne had its heyday in Edward I's reign when the great king came here to visit Roger de Leybourne in his castle; Roger was a fellow-Crusader and a notable warrior. The fragments of medieval wall tucked under the wing of a modern house behind the church probably belong to a later building. It would be nice to believe the tradition that the two votive crowns which hang in the church were given by the King and Queen. If this is too much to swallow, you may at least accept that the heart-shrine

in the N. chapel with its two stone caskets contains the heart of Sir Roger. Much of what meets the eye in the church comes from a drastic late-Victorian restoration.

A little stream which trundles along the valley from Addington here turns N. towards the Medway and is turned by gravel workings into a chain of ponds. These are a favoured haunt of waterfowl and repay an extended visit.

LINTON—*on greensand ridge S. of Maidstone.*

Horace Walpole came here to visit his friend Galfridus Mann at Linton Place and said that he had all Kent for his garden. This is the impression one still gets from the footpath which passes behind Mann's massive white house. It is one of the great Kentish views. The footpath starts in the churchyard, past the church which has been restored beyond recognition. It is full of monuments to Manns and later Cornwallises, some of them very good and all interesting illustrations of the change in monumental fashions. The village, built on the steep side of the hill, has a few good houses, the best of them the pub, and a pretty ragstone row of almshouses set across the face of the church.

Because of the slope Linton has no room to grow. The new population is over the crest of the hill, at Coxheath. The heath, site of a great militia camp during the Napoleonic invasion scare, has vanished entirely.

LITTLEBOURNE—*in valley of the Little Stour E. of Canterbury.*

A large village around cross roads on the Sandwich road. The Little Stour is a clear stream which mirrors a large watermill N. of the village. Near here is the big 13th-century church. For once the most attractive part of the village is on the main road where a dignified 18th century brick house, some homely cottages and a group of oasts stand around a small green with the river just beyond.

At Lee Abbey, a celebrated Gothic house now demolished, Sir Egerton Brydges established one of the private presses with which the art of fine printing was revived in the 18th century.

LOOSE—*in greensand country S. of Maidstone.*
The Loose valley which used to be one of the most exquisite parts of Kent is largely ruined now by injudicious development and neglect. The little River Loose which has a habit of losing itself by burrowing underground trickles sadly through the sad scene. On its banks, below the village, stands Hayle Mill from which the finest handmade paper in the world comes.

Loose village sits in the narrowest part of the valley with hills rising abruptly on both sides. Here the river comes into its own, dividing to provide a very nice raised causeway and cascading in a number of mill-races. The sound of water is everywhere. The scene at the bridge is enchanting. Here are some good houses, some of the 18th century, some, like the Wool House (National Trust but not open) from two centuries earlier. The church looks well in this crowded setting but is almost completely a Victorian rebuilding.

LOWER HALSTOW—*on eastern shore of Medway estuary.*
The great wetlands of the Medway marshes spread for miles, the home or resting place of innumerable birds. The coast is deeply indented with salt-water creeks and on one of these stands Lower Halstow. Not a tourist place, but for those with a taste for communities set on the edge of worlds an evocative one. All the coast around is fascinating with its memories of past seafarers, who buried their dead on Deadman's Island and put their sick in the ill-fated lazaret on Chetney Island, and of Francis Drake who learnt his seamanship in these tricky tidal waters when his father was vicar of Upchurch.

Right on the creek stands a neat little church whose tower

provides the only positive accent in the place. The core of the building is Saxon, enlarged and transformed in the 13th century and again a century or more later. The clear-glass windows look out on to creek and estuary. Here is a famous treasure, a small Norman tub-font, lead with elegantly moulded arcades. This was hidden under cement until vibrations from naval gunnery out in the river cracked it and showed what lay within.

LUDDESDOWNE—*in North Downs S. of Watling Street and Cobham.*

A very small village in fine downland. It is the hub of a web of field and downland tracks. Looking across to the tower of the church and its attendant manor, there is no hint of London, barely 25 miles away, or of the nearby chimneys of Thameside cement works.

Here survives in ground plan an unchanged settlement. It looks so perfect that the closer view is a disappointment. The church was restored to the very limit of endurance in mid-Victorian times. The Court, next to the church, is of genuine antiquity, late Norman or early 13th century, but its aspect is rather gaunt and grim.

LULLINGSTONE—*in Darent valley.*

The Darent valley was a favoured part of Kent in Roman times, and here on a shelf above the river (a much bigger stream then than now) a Romanized British landowner built his house in the 1st century. The site was discovered after the War and the remains were excavated scientifically. The site is now open to the public, giving the most interesting and exciting glimpse into Romano-British domestic life which Kent—or indeed the whole country—affords. There are spectacular mosaic floors, a pagan chapel, and—rarest of all—a Christian chapel with painted walls.

Beyond the road to the Roman villa is Lullingstone Castle (limited openings in Summer). Not a castle at all but a lovely 18th-century house reconstructed from a Tudor mansion, of which the deep-red brick gatehouse remains. The setting is lovely. Across the lawn from the house is Lullingstone Church, a medieval building transformed in the early 18th century, so that it is the most intriguing blend of medieval and Georgian. Superb plaster-work. The rood-screen, which had only been completed a decade or so when the Reformation made it obsolete, is particularly elegant. The monuments, to Peches and Harts who successively occupied the castle, are worthy of this beautiful setting.

LYDD—*on Romney Marsh.*
Lydd is one of the two ancient boroughs of the Marsh and still, in 1972, retains the splendid trappings of power, including Mayor and Corporation and status as a major limb of the Cinque Port of Romney. Before the River Rother went elsewhere it ran into the sea here and Lydd stood on a pebbly promontary in the estuary. Now the town is two miles inland, and the sea recedes daily through the build-up of shingle at Dungeness. It is a small town but a very large parish which takes in Dungeness Point and all the shingle wastes as far as the Sussex border.

Lydd offers those contrasts which bring home to the visitor the essential flavour of history. A place of village size with borough status, an ancient sea port without the sea which contains an airport and a nuclear power-station, the home of Lyddite explosives and a great bird observatory; the list of incongruities seems endless. There is much pleasure in walking around the neatly laid-out streets of the medieval town, set about the great church, and in finding the occasional notable buildings among the humble. The church is magnificent, a great building with Saxon fragments and a noble 15th century tower. This latter is possibly the finest in Kent apart from the cathedral. Note how well it dominates the town; note, too, inside, the lovely vaulting which you see as you look up from the entrance. The sanctuary was destroyed by enemy action during the War and the present lovely tall lancets are modern and entirely satisfactory.

Lydd has surely the biggest village green in Kent, a large expanse called the Ripe (literally the strip). Beyond this there is a thin band of housing and then the pebbles stretch to the horizon. In the distance are the massive blocks of the power-station and the slim lines of the old and new lighthouses. There is an exhilarating drive in this direction, passing the bird observatory and the Warden's wind-beaten cottage on the way, and seeing an abundance of sea-birds in the flooded gravel-workings. Beyond is the track of the little railway, the coastguards' cottages, and then the awful thin line of holiday bungalows unbroken along the front from Dungeness to Littlestone.

LYMINGE—*at head of Elham Valley N.W. of Folkestone.*
This is much the largest place in the valley and much of the recent growth is not very sightly. It could never have been as attractive as Elham and Barham and now the village as you pass through on the main road is decidedly unattractive. Its charms and its history lie away from the road.

Here was one of the earliest Christian foundations after St Augustine's arrival. King Ethelbert of Kent's daughter Ethelburga founded an abbey at Lyminge in 633 and she became the first abbess. The abbey did not survive the Norman Conquest but the abbey church, largely rebuilt by St Dunstan in the 10th century, forms the fabric of the present parish church. It is the most substantial Saxon church in Kent. The tower, which is what one sees first, is misleading for it is a Tudor addition. On the N. side there can be seen outside an excavated tomb which stood in the earlier building; this is said to have been the grave of the most celebrated woman saint of Saxon times, Mildred. But what was she doing here? Her abbey was at Minster-in-Thanet.

LYMPNE—*above Romney Marsh W. of Hythe.*
In Roman times Lympne stood on the estuary of the River Limen (later Rother) and the Roman Portus Lemanis was inferior only to Richborough and Dover among Channel ports. Later a Saxon Shore fort was built to guard the vulnerable coast. Then the Limen silted up and the port slowly died. The Roman buildings were robbed for building materials; among other things for a church built higher up the cliff by the Norman Archbishop Lanfranc. With the shifting of the unstable cliffs the ruins of the Roman fort were tumbled into chaos. The average visitor can make nothing of them but they have a certain fascination. Stutfall Castle, as the Roman fort is now called, can be seen from a steep footpath which drops from the village to the Royal Military Canal. It marks the beginning of Stone Street which heads, mostly dead straight, for Canterbury.

In the 11th century Lympne became a manor of the Archdeacons of Canterbury (the young Thomas Becket held this office) who had their hall beside the church. During the Hundred Years War this was rebuilt and fortified as a coastal defence. This is the building, much restored and extended early this century, which may be visited today. There is a superb view of Romney Marsh from the leads of the tower. Lympne Castle is best viewed from the footpath to Stutfall Castle.

The church is a little disappointing, apart from the massive central tower which dates from Lanfranc's foundation.

From this N.E. corner of the old coast there are some of the best of the views of Romney Marsh. Along the minor road eastwards one comes to Shepway Cross, traditional site of the meetings of the Court of Shepway where the legal business of the Cinque Ports was transacted. The cross is modern (1923) and remarkably fine; the view S.W. from it is even finer.

There are many good walks at Lympne, most of which take in the Royal Military Canal. One climbs up from the Canal to the little hamlet of Court-at-Street where there is an inn with a jolly sign. Just behind the ridge here are the remains of the chapel of Bellerica, which was the scene of poor Elizabeth Barton's 'visions'; she was the Holy Maid of Kent who opposed Henry VIII's divorce and suffered for it.

MAIDSTONE—*on the Medway.*

The County Town. It is not very clear how Maidstone superseded the ancient capital, Canterbury. The shire court was probably held on Penenden Heath from late Saxon times and this remained the centre of legal administration until a new Sessions House was built more conveniently in the town early in the 19th century. Meanwhile the position at a crossing of the river brought prosperity to Maidstone which increased when it became a centre for the cloth trade in the 15th century. The Archbishop's patronage helped too.

Maidstone is now busy, noisy, largely ugly. Its function as administrative capital, industrial town, market town, shopping centre, is too much to be performed within the pattern of medieval streets. Most recent changes have helped to destroy its character and its charm.

For the visitor there remains an incomparable group of ancient buildings upstream from the bridge. The eye-catcher is the Archbishop's Palace, originally 14th century but now largely Tudor, in stone and half-timbering. Municipally owned and mostly put to rather unworthy uses. Next comes All Saints, a great piece of late 14th century architectural arrogance, more worldly than godly but very splendid with its great windows and its collegiate trappings. This was built by

Archbishop Courtenay in Richard II's reign to go with his newly founded college of priests next door. Courtenay wanted to be buried here, but the King, who had been afraid of him alive, overruled the dead Primate and buried him splendidly in the Cathedral. Of the college there are fine remains, notably the great gatehouse with vaulted arch and the Master's house. The buildings are now used as the County Music Centre. Over the road from this noble group of buildings is the barn or stables of the palace, a superb stone and timbered hall now housing a museum of carriages.

Everything else in Maidstone is anti-climax after this. Just

Maidstone: Mote Park

Next page: Maidstone—All Saints Church and College

over the bridge, in a squalid setting, is St Peter's, a fragment of a 13th century hospital chapel rather clumsily turned into a church in early Victorian times. Near the opposite bank of the river the hall of the Guild of Corpus Christi, of early 15th century, is incorporated in offices of a brewery. There are a few good houses of 17th–18th century dates in Earl Street and by the market buildings there survives miraculously an unspoilt dissenters' chapel, the Unitarian Church built in 1730 and still in use. The very good museum—by far the best in Kent—is housed in an Elizabethan town house on which various additions, some of them interesting, have been tacked. (At the back, for example, is the re-erected half-timbered Court Lodge from East Farleigh.) A few old houses survive among the supermarkets in Week Street, the principal shopping street, and rather more in Bank Street, a narrow lane behind the High Street. One could go on with the catalogue of the things which are worth a second look, but it would not amount to a lot. The town had a small architectural revival in the early 19th century under a local architect John Whichcord—the disused church of Holy Trinity, between two hospitals, was his—but recent additions to the scene are mainly either stodgy or vulgar.

Lest this seem too discouraging, Maidstone stands in the middle of fine country. The river, upstream to Farleigh and down to Allington, is mostly lovely and untainted by the town. To the E. the River Len avoids most of the urban sprawl and its waters are tapped to form the magnificent artificial lake of Mote Park. This former seat of Lord Romney—the house is now a Cheshire Home—is an outstandingly lovely example of 18th century landscaping. It is owned by the town and sporting and other recreational uses have not been allowed to spoil the prospects to the Downs, the timber, and the elegant temple of 1801 and the solid ragstone boathouses.

West Malling

MALLING—*to the W. of Maidstone.*
There are two Mallings. East Malling is a small village now overwhelmed by extensive housing estates. Before the commuters transformed it, its *raison d'être* was the Horticultural Research Station, which does work of international importance in the improvement of strains of fruit. The headquarters are housed in Bradbourne, a great house—not open but visible from the road—which was the seat of the celebrated Kentish family of Twisden. The present house is largely of early 18th century. The church is set prettily at the end of a short closed road with contrasted houses, one a typical Kentish hall-house, another elegant and restrained in 18th century brick; it is large, tall and light from a clerestorey—comparatively rare in Kentish churches. For the rest East Malling has one or two pleasant

walks to offer, and a glimpse, on the way to West Malling, of the very elegant late 18th century mansion, Clare House, with its jolly little dome.

West Malling is larger, a town to East Malling's village, and much more complicated in history and layout. Here is a high street to match the best in the South-East—but so cluttered with traffic that it is difficult to appreciate it. Narrowed at one end and closed by a sudden change of direction at the other it is like an elongated square rather than a street. At the S. end is the church, largely rebuilt but not badly and with many good things, especially rich Royal Arms of James II and an extraordinary garish Jacobean monument to a Brett.

Gundulf, the formidable Norman Bishop of Rochester, had an interest in Malling. He founded an abbey here, of which substantial remains, including a late Norman tower and a handsome 15th century gatehouse, are incorporated in the present buildings which belong to an Anglican religious order and are not open. Gundulf was the leading military architect of his day, and he was responsible too for St Leonard's Tower, a half-mile along the Tonbridge Road. This must be one of the earliest stone castles put up after the Conquest and is of the greatest interest. It is open regularly to visitors.

Between the Tower and the town is the Manor House, early Victorian on an 18th century base, poised on a bank with a pretty lake below and separated from it by the main road. This is now an hotel.

MARDEN—*in the low Weald.*

A large village and an important factor in the agriculture of the Weald. It is the centre of the apple country and important for hops too. Although commuters have settled here it has not become, like Staplehurst, suburbanized, but has kept its essentially rural quality. The shops are country shops, the people countrymen. The buildings are appropriately homely. Even the church, with an endearingly comical tower, is unassuming, apart from some powerful, uncharacteristic modern glass. The stocks in the churchyard help to maintain the mood, and so do the weatherboard fronts in the little square.

The country around is equally unpretentious, and equally pleasing. A bit of genuine Kent.

MARGATE—*on Thanet.*

The largest of the Thanet resorts. There are several Margates: the Margate of Dreamland and the amusement arcades, the Margate of the Cliftonville hotels, the residents' Margate where the semis merge with the wide cornfields of Thanet.

The town had medieval origins and it had some status as a minor partner of Dover in the Cinque Ports. The old church, with its large collection of 15th and 16th century brasses, is a reminder of this. But Margate came into its own with the fashion of sea-bathing. It was the first Kentish resort and that curious device the bathing-machine made its début on Margate sands. The big hospital on the left as one approaches the town centre is still called the Royal Sea Bathing Hospital and still occupies its original Regency buildings. Parts of the central Cecil Square belong to this heyday too, although much has sadly been destroyed.

The surprises of Margate lie outside the central area. These include of course the Grotto, the most extraordinary of its kind in the country; a shell-encrusted series of chalk caverns, highly fantastical and with legends to match. But it is surely an expression of that whimsical spirit which produced the above-ground follies of 18th-century Thanet, Kingsgate Castle and its attendant towers and temples. With Salmeston Grange inland, we are on more conventional ground; this was a manor of St Augustine's Abbey, Canterbury, and a remarkably complete range of medieval buildings it is too. There is a medieval fantasy farther S.W. in Garlinge, where the new houses have as neighbour the magnificent flint and brick gate-house of a fortified 15th century house. The home of the Daundelyons has gone and only this Dent-de-Lion Gate remains of their greatness.

One goes to Margate not for these ancient memories but for candyfloss or conferences and for the extraordinary Thanet air which has a bouquet found nowhere else in Kent.

MEDWAY, RIVER—*the central river of Kent.*
The Medway rises in Sussex in a number of streams coming out of the sandy hills below Turners Hill. It enters Kent near Ashurst, collects its first considerable tributary—the Eden—at Penshurst and flows through the wide Wealden plain past Tonbridge and Yalding. Here it passes through a narrow gap in the greensand hills to Maidstone, then turns N. to pass through the Downs to Rochester, and so to the sea at Queenborough. It is tidal from Allington.

Bridges on the Medway: Teston

Bridges on the Medway: Farleigh

In 1741 the river was made navigable to canal traffic between Allington and Tonbridge, and it is still extensively used for commercial purposes up to Maidstone. It has also become very popular with pleasure craft. A legacy of the old 'Navigation' is the towpath which provides a long-distance footpath, practically continuous from Aylesford to Tonbridge; it passes through some of the loneliest country in the South-East.

MEOPHAM—*in North Downs S. of Gravesend.*
A very long village stretching along the main Gravesend–Tonbridge road for more than three miles. It has grown rapidly in recent years through the incursion of commuters, who have helped to make it one of the most lively and self-conscious of villages. No place has a firmer regard for such amenities as rights-of-way.

Kent merges with Sussex, near Ashurst in the Upper Medway Valley

The countryside around is very lovely. Meopham itself is good in bits. There is a magnificent church, standing back from the road on the northern edge of the old village. The building is more of a piece than is usual, and that belonging to the early 14th century. Some good fittings, too, notably the pulpit. Next best in Meopham is the Green, where cricket is played. There is a smock mill opposite and some sightly cottages. To the N.E. Camer Park is a pleasantly landscaped estate around a formal mansion.

The local society's guides to footpath walks are a model of their kind; they make a good investment and help the visitor to get on the right terms with this enchanting downland country.

MEREWORTH—*in greensand country between Maidstone and Tonbridge.*

From a distance the village looks odd, its signpost being a solidly-classical stone spire which is quite alien to this landscape. At closer range the village pattern seems alien, too, as if it has been planted by design. It had. The medieval village lay a half-mile to the E., right on the site which John Fane, later Earl of Westmorland, fancied for his new house. So the village was moved along the road, and in its place arose Mereworth Castle.

Nothing could be less like a castle. The house, dating from the 1720s, is an imaginative copy by Colen Campbell of an Italian villa by the 16th century master Palladio. No longer open to the public, it can be glimpsed through the lodge gates, from which it can be seen that the improbably long odds came off and that this alien palace looks very well in its English parkland setting. Go round the park by a lane which leads to East Peckham church and you will see the great triumphal arch which closes the view from the rear of the house.

The new church, whose tower is an echo of St Martin's-in-the-Fields, is most exciting, a great classical hall which gives an impression of richness without elaboration or fuss. Monuments from the old church are tucked away at the back where their robust vigour does not conflict with the general austerity.

On the lane to West Peckham there is a good view of another great house, Yotes Court (gardens sometimes open). This was built just before the Restoration and so makes a nice contrast to Groombridge Place, of about the same date. Yotes Court is lighter and more symmetrical. Standing beyond the great trees of the park it seems one of the most desirable houses in Kent, big enough to be impressive, not enough to be oppressive.

To the N. Mereworth Woods, a vast tract of old and new plantations which offer several walks surprising in their interest and variety.

MERSHAM—*E. of Ashford.*

The East Stour flows just S. of the village. This is a country of gentle fields and scattered good houses. The best of the village is around the church, where there is a handsome Court Lodge in stone, largely medieval. The church is a solid Norman building with some surprising additions, notably a huge late 14th century W. window with tracery which is—to say the least—original. The monuments are to Knatchbulls, including Sir Wyndham who commissioned Robert Adam to rebuild his country house just before his death in 1763. The house—Mersham-le-Hatch—lies across the A20 behind magnificent trees. It is a solid plain brick block with linked wings, in admirable and slightly dull good taste. The Knatchbulls, later Knatchbull-Hugessons—one was a nephew of Jane Austen—and now Lords Brabourne, have left, and the house is a home for deprived children which does admirable work.

MILSTED—*in North Downs S.E. of Sittingbourne.*

You almost see Milsted from the M2, but happily the scurry-

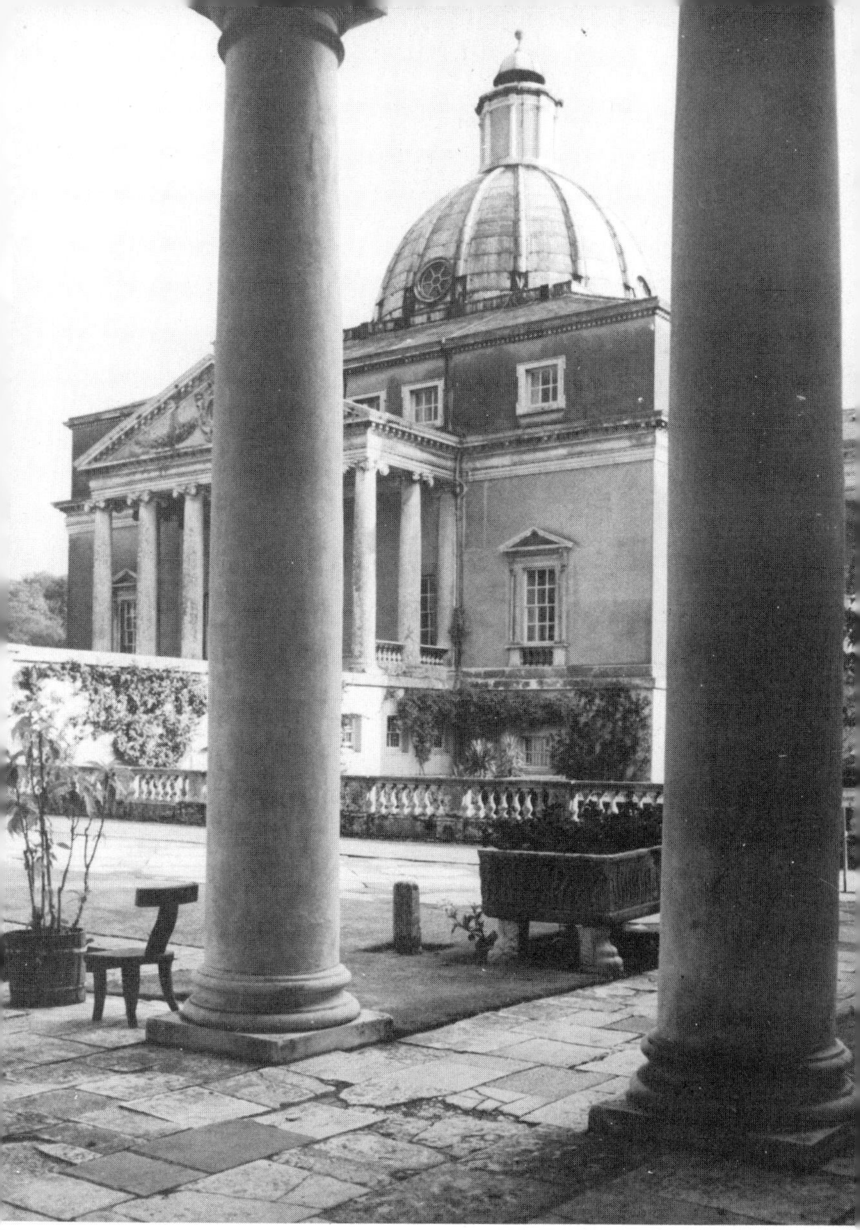

Mereworth Castle

ing cars are trapped on the motorway and cannot escape to explore the delights of the village. The lanes here are narrow and winding, and the approach is necessarily sedate.

This village is high in my Top Twenty, not for any special distinction in its buildings or setting but because everything is to the right scale and there are no discordant notes. The very lack of high-spots is an asset. The church for example is very ordinary, having suffered the usual devastating restoration of the 1870's. Don't look too closely but notice how well it fills its corner of the village, with a Kentish hall-house across its line. Opposite there is a larger half-timbered manor-house half-hidden behind its protective wall.

MILTON REGIS—see *Sittingbourne*.

MINSTER—*there are two Minsters in Kent, one on each of the principal islands and with histories closely related.*

MINSTER-IN-SHEPPEY—*on the central ridge of Sheppey.* The Minster—a Saxon nunnery—was founded by Sexburga, whose husband was King of Kent and a grandson of Ethelbert, so that it was in direct line from St Augustine. This was in 664. She became abbess and in due time died and was canonized. Parts of the northern side of the church perhaps belong to this original abbey-church. It was in a terribly vulnerable position, being visible from the sea, and Danish raiders destroyed the abbey and killed the nuns. The house was refounded by the Normans. The parish church existed side by side with the nunnery, so that the existing N. aisle was the abbey, the present nave belonged to the parish. There are interesting and intriguing architectural details. Of the many monuments the most celebrated is that of Sir Robert de Shurland, with a swimming horse behind his effigy. Readers of *The Ingoldsby Legends* will know the answer to this riddle, even if it is the wrong answer! There is a delightful monument to Sir Thomas

Cheyne, who appears in that fascinating Elizabethan play *Arden of Feversham*. Of the other buildings of the abbey only a big 15th century gatehouse remains.

The position of the abbey is still fine, giving long views inland across the Swale. Minster village is shabby and there are undistinguished housing estates nearly all the way to Sheerness.

MINSTER-IN-THANET—*on low ground in the Wantsum valley.*

The abbey here came five years after Sheppey's. It was founded by Egbert, King of Kent, as an act of penance, and his niece Domneva became the first abbess. Her daughter Mildred succeeded her and raised the house's reputation high by her firm rule and her personal sanctity. She was canonized and buried in the abbey church, but the miracles attributed to her stopped short of protecting the abbey from attack. The Danes destroyed it utterly. St Mildred's bones were rescued by Canute who, in repayment for the damage done by his countrymen, gave them splendid reburial in St Augustine's Abbey, Canterbury. The abbey, unlike Sheppey's was not revived by the Normans. The lands were acquired by St Augustine's and an abbey grange was established in the village to administer the estate. This is the present Minster Abbey, whose ancient buildings became the home of Benedictine nuns in our own day. They are large and complex and well worth the visit.

Over the road from the present abbey is the parish church, which is astonishingly large and majestic, big enough to be the abbey-church it never was. Presumably the particular favour of the abbots of St Augustine's accounts for its splendour. It is nearly all late Norman and Early English, developed from an earlier building. The stone vault is new, from Victorian times, but it merely carries out the original designer's intentions. The choir stalls survive intact from the early 15th century, together with an extremely good set of misericords. They are all different, and all help to draw aside the curtain which separates us from the past.

There is not much else in the village—and indeed it would be greedy to ask for more. A visit might be rounded off, on a fine day, by a walk across Minster Marshes to the banks of the Wantsum. Out in these flats, where even the giant towers of Richborough power station are cut down to scale, it is not difficult to visualize the old deep-water channel which made Thanet an island. The earth wall which follows the present channel was the work of the abbots in controlling the flood waters over their land.

NETTLESTEAD—*in Medway gap through the greensand hills.*

Half of the village is merged with Wateringbury, and the other half is at Nettlestead Green to the S.W. Between the two the middle reaches of the Medway are at their loveliest around Nettlestead Place. Here is an extremely attractive group of medieval buildings. The stone-built Place may be largely rebuilt—although it retains its 13th century undercroft, but it is certainly a very delightful house set about with rose- and water-gardens (occasionally open). The house is approached through an absurdly small fortified gatehouse. Immediately adjacent to the house on the N. is the church, which was largely rebuilt by the Pympes who lived here in the 15th century. The work was clearly done as an exercise in glass. The nave windows are out of proportion in this little building and they are filled with splendid glass, some of it original. The benefactor celebrates in them the glories of his family, his friends and his age.

For a view showing the relationship of church and Place take the lane across Wateringbury Bridge and look down from the summit of Bow Hill. A lovely prospect.

NEWCHURCH—*on Romney Marsh.*

An inland parish of the Marsh, just an inn and a group of cottages dominated by the mass of the great church. Notice how this is raised above the dead level of the Marsh on a low mound. Inside it is a gaunt barn, suited to performance of plays and music—but who would come? A good 15th century font. I prefer the exterior, its ragstone mellowed by five centuries of marshland cold and damp, and the high tower with its gargoyles looking across the levels.

NEWENDEN—*on Sussex border in Rother valley.*

The last village in Kent. The river boundary is only yards away. The dominant building in the little village is the inn. Opposite is an odd-looking church which illustrates the waywardness of a variety of restorers. Inside there is one of the finest of Norman fonts, a massive square stone bowl adorned with low-relief carvings of beasties real and mythological.

The Rother here flows in a narrow flat valley. There is a riverside walk downstream towards Rolvenden, and a short diversion by the way takes in the earthworks of Castle Toll. This is an early Norman motte standing in older embankments sometimes—and rather absurdly—identified as the Roman Anderida. Most people would say that this was at Pevensey.

NEWINGTON-NEXT-FOLKESTONE—*just outside Cheriton to the W.*

Travellers on the A20 catch a glimpse of the little belfried church to the N. of the road, but few stop to look at this remarkably complete Norman church. It makes a pretty picture in the tiny village. A little to the W. is a hamlet, Frogholt, with some good houses and a little roadside stream.

The North Downs rise sharply above the village. A narrow steep lane to Paddlesworth gives one of the best of Kentish views. The land drops spectacularly to the W. providing a dramatic prospect of the escarpment and the levels of Romney Marsh to the left.

NEWINGTON-NEXT-SITTINGBOURNE—*on Watling Street E. of Medway towns.*

Apart from an old coaching inn there is nothing to catch the eye on the main road and the side road down to the station is no better. Come here when the cherry is in flower, around the beginning of May, and it is another story. Beyond the railway the acres of the cherry orchards are set out like a great white sea. Floating in the billows is the tower of Newington church, making a picture instantly recognized as pure Kentish. It is a church to examine in detail too. Notice the elaborate wooden cover of the font, elegant Tudor woodwork. Also, a rarity in any parish church, a saint's shrine. St Robert was buried in a chapel on the pilgrim's road, and after the end of the Canterbury pilgrimages his shrine was re-erected here.

NEW ROMNEY—*the capital of Romney Marsh.*

This was one of the original Cinque Ports. It stood on the estuary of the River Rother with a wide bay looking across to the pebbly shore of Dungeness. The river mouth began to close up in the 13th century through piled shingle and river silt; then in 1287 the end came dramatically. In a great storm the mouth was blocked and the river found a new outlet to the sea below Rye. New Romney declined gently but retained the trappings of its former glory, its status as a Cinque Port and its Mayor and Corporation. It still has them. Today it is a minor shopping centre and holiday resort (the sands at Littlestone are excellent at the right state of the tide) and the little Romney, Hythe and Dymchurch railway attracts visitors.

The town is set out on a grid system which gives it a formality rare in an ancient settlement. Most of the outward appearance is of the 18th century; not many of the houses are distinguished, but there is an air of quiet refinement. Apart from the church there are no tourist attractions. St John's Priory has a medieval core but the wall to the street is an obvious hotchpotch of broken fragments. Of three medieval churches only one remains, but that is of major importance. The great Norman tower—its truncated spire looks just a little odd—is surely the finest in Kent. Inside is a big three-aisled hall, open and light. Rebuilders in the 13th century did not get much beyond the chancel and so the massive late Norman nave piers survive intact. Following common medieval practice the nave was used as the original town hall, and New Romney still makes its mayor each year at the tomb of Richard Stuppenye.

New Romney makes a good base for the exploration of the Marsh. The town does not sprawl and one can be in marshland in minutes. Along the Ashford road there are ruins, on a typical Marsh mound, of the four corners of Hope All Saints church, all that is left of a lost village. Where the Appledore road turns sharp left just outside the town, a good short walk may be had on the old road to Old Romney, which gives an accurate impression of this strange and strangely attractive country.

NORTHFLEET—*on Thameside W. of Gravesend.*

Hardly tourist country, but there is some interest here. The original settlement can still be identified among all the brick and concrete. Here is a church with Saxon fabric embedded in a handsome 14th century structure. The rood screen survives. While we are looking at churches there are three others, two in Victorian Gothic, at Rosherville and Perry Street, and a most impressive Roman Catholic church in brick on the best site in the town; this is by Sir Giles Gilbert Scott at his most confident.

Nothing remains of Rosherville Gardens, created by the enterprising Jeremiah Rosher in the 1830s. These were plea-

Downland Kent: The Stour Gap from above Wye

sure gardens with music, lights and a zoo, which made a favourite outing from Victorian London.

NORTH DOWNS—*The principal landscape feature of Kent.* The chalk hills, with steep escarpments to the S. and many dry valleys on the N., cross the whole county from Westerham to Dover. The wall is broken in only three places, by the river gaps of the Darent, Medway and Stour. The proposed (and partially completed) North Downs Way is only one of many tracks which enable walkers to get to know this country better than motorists can hope to do.

Downland Kent: Lees Park, Sheldwich

OFFHAM—*in greensand country S.W. of Maidstone.*
Offham's fame rests on the possession of a quintain, the only one surviving in the country. This was a device to train eye and hand for sport and war. This venerable and much renewed relic stands on a highly picturesque green backed by fine houses in brick and stone. The church is well to the N., alone except for a farm. It is basically Norman and pleasing in a homely way. The setting is lovely with long views to the Downs.

Paths lead from the village into Mereworth Woods, or across farmland to Mereworth, or eastwards by field and wood to Malling. All very well worth sampling.

OLD ROMNEY—*on Romney Marsh.*

This stood farther up the estuary than New Romney and had a share in the prosperity of its neighbour. In its day it had three parish churches. Now there is one and very little else, and the sea is far away. Old Romney is one of the smallest of Kentish villages and one of the most charming. The church on its minute hillock, framed by old trees and with a lamb-scattered pasture in front, is a scene to be long remembered. Behind the church, where the old road goes through to New Romney, are a few cottages and the manor house. The church will already be familiar to those who saw the films about Doctor Syn. Utterly without architectural pretensions, it is a pattern for all homely village churches, with its text-boards, Royal Arms, box pews and western choir gallery. The glass is clear, and one looks out to green pastures. Although it is in excellent repair, there is an endearing air of gentle decay.

On the seaward side of the main road to New Romney one sees, as little more than a shadow picked out by the evening sun, the line of the Rhee Wall by which the reclamation of the Marsh was accelerated.

OLD SOAR—see *Plaxtol.*

OSPRINGE—*on Watling Street just W. of Faversham.*

This was a sizable place in Roman times and important finds have been made here. Then followed the Canterbury pilgrims and the coaching age, then the modern age of heavy traffic which threatened to shake the place to bits. Now, with the opening of the M2 a little peace has come to Ospringe. At the corner of Water Lane—which until very recent time lived up to its name because a nailbourne flowed along it—is the Maison Dieu, two fragments of a pilgrim's hostel and hospital founded early in the 13th century. The main building is open

(D of E) and has some local antiquities on show. The church is farther up the lane and quite detached from the village. The rather grotesque Victorian tower—a conspicuous feature from the motorway—is misleading for this is a largely Norman building. Large alabaster monument to a Jacobean worthy.

OTFORD—*in Holmesdale N. of Sevenoaks.*
One of the few villages which lie actually along the Pilgrims Way. It is at the head of the Darent gap and there is a delightful walk down the valley to Shoreham. Otford is still pretty in spite of heavy traffic. The cross-roads are marked by a large pond with the village green beyond, flanked by the church and a few very good houses. Altogether an attractive scene. The curious ruined brick tower in the background is all that remains of a palace of the Archbishops, rebuilt in Henry VIII's reign but quickly abandoned. There are legends about Becket who had trouble here in his early days. The church has some early work and a little interest has survived a drastic restoration. Notable for grand and grandiose monuments to members of the Polhill family.

The village grows rapidly, but fortunately most of the new is to the E., leaving the old village almost untouched.

OTHAM—*in greensand country E. of Maidstone.*
The tide of Maidstone flows ever nearer, but still Otham retains its charm. Few villages have more fine houses from the age of wool. Stoneacre (NT) is the largest, but this is cheating because early in this century Aymer Vallance added bits and pieces from other houses to the original. Synyards has had an upper floor inserted in the hall, but it is still a good specimen of a Kentish Yeoman's house of early Tudor times. Wardes, rather less easily seen from the road, is older and has a big 16th century addition. The church is away to the W. It has a pretty spire but restoration has destroyed much of its

interest. The Len flows below the village, and a battered weatherboarded mill stands beside the lane to Bearsted. There are attractive views, especially from the green.

OTTERDEN—*in North Downs between Faversham and Lenham.*
Lovely rolling country, but where is the village? Nothing here but mansion and church, companionably together in the park. The Place, now turned into very superior apartments, is a small Tudor house blown up large in Victorian days, pleasing in its red brick dress. Under its shadow is a neat little plain church, utterly unassuming outside, rebuilt from a medieval original in mid-18th century. The inside is equally plain apart from the matchless collection of monuments to former owners of the house.

OXNEY, ISLE OF—*between Weald and Marsh.*
The island is a low whale-back hill between two arms of the River Rother. There are two villages, at Wittersham and Stone. Good viewpoints between the two, looking inland, and from beyond Stone over Romney Marsh.

PADDLESWORTH—*two villages of this name.*
1. In East Kent, on North Downs behind Folkestone, a lonely early Norman church, its nearest neighbour an inn with a name—Cat and Custard Pot—derived from Surtees. Pleasant wooded country to the N. with walks.
2. In West Kent, between the Medway at Snodland and the Downs. Again a very small Norman church, until recently used as a barn. Here is a perfect example of an early Saxon settlement, with church, manor, farm and cottages probably on the original sites of their Saxon prototypes. The whole set off by fine trees. It looks well from the Downs.

PATRIXBOURNE—*in valley of Little Stour E. of Canterbury.* This looks too good to be true, and in a sense it isn't. Those pretty Tudor cottages are mostly Victorian but so nicely done that one readily forgives the deception. They are set casually along a narrow winding street. In the heart of the village an incredibly splendid late Norman church. Very like neighbouring Barfreston and probably from the same stable. The S. door, a little less exquisite in detail than Barfreston's, is on an even more ambitious scale. Like Barfreston too there is a S.E. priest's door of the same date. The body of the church is larger than Barfreston and with more later work in evidence, but the E. wheel window is comparable.

PECKHAM—*neighbouring parishes in the low Weald between Tonbridge and Maidstone.*
1. East Peckham is now a large sprawling village in the flat country where the River Bourne joins the Medway. Branbridges, where the main road crosses the river, was the business heart of the Medway Navigation. There are some delightful cottages here and there, but the village has grown too much and too fast. The old church is more than a mile away on the greensand, with a superb view from the lychgate. Not many churches have a finer setting. It is a pity the old building has been so badly mauled in restoration. There are monuments to the Twysdens of Roydon, the Tudor Hall just below the hill. This is much altered by extensive Victorian additions, but still has its original terraced garden with brick wall and corner turrets, rather like those at Hales Place in Tenterden. The smaller Little Roydon opposite is more immediately pleasing, a very charming early Georgian mansion. The landscape is delightful, but threatening notices forbid closer acquaintance.
2. From Church Hill you look across the valley to West Peckham. Here is a little gem of a village with a big open green, an inn and a small church which proclaims its Saxon

origins with a deep splayed tower window. It is a dark, evocative building whose main interest lies in the N. chapel which became the family pew of the Bartholomews. Here lies Leonard Bartholomew, a Georgian gentleman impressive in his marble wig. All the fittings are of great interest.

The houses around the green are of no particular merit, but along the lane towards Mereworth is Duke's Place, a great rambling timber-framed house which is on the site of, and may in fact have been the original, preceptory of the Knights Hospitallers. It is certainly a gorgeous sight.

West Peckham is a centre for some excellent walks, taking in to the W. the park of Oxenhoath, a large and eccentric mansion in a beautiful setting, and to the N.W. the greensand heights of Gover Hill (NT) from which the usual ranging view of the Weald is enlivened by the formal parkland in the foreground.

PEMBURY—*in Weald N.E. of Tunbridge Wells.*
Now virtually a suburb of Tunbridge Wells. Much of the village lies along the main Hastings road, awaiting the relief of a bypass. In this area is the triangular Upper Green, facing the Camden Arms—Bayham Abbey, the home of the Marquis Camden, is not far away—and a beautifully sited Victorian Gothic church. The rest is concentrated at Lower Green (but the green itself has gone) where there is nothing of interest. Detached from both greens the old church is down a narrow lane to the W. where it has for company only a mansion which now houses a girls' public school. This is a pretty corner, even if the church—Norman with 14th century additions and 19th century manglings—is of limited interest. This is Culpeper country, although they spelled it Colepeper in these parts. The country beyond the church towards Capel is wooded and most pleasing, and there is also some fine rolling landscape beyond the new church towards the Sussex border.

Penshurst Place

PENSHURST—*in upper Medway valley S.W. of Tonbridge.*

A village of outstanding interest. There is much to be seen quite apart from the incomparable Penshurst Place. The great house, which from the park displays a late 16th and 19th century face, is fundamentally a great medieval hall house, built by a London merchant-prince in the reign of Edward III. No space here for a catalogue of its splendours, which are innumerable. The house, already much enlarged, came in 1552 to the Sidneys who own it still. Here Philip Sidney, pattern of Elizabethans, was born and here he oversaw the updating of the buildings to give a Renaissance flavour to their medievalism.

The village looks perfectly Tudor and is in fact mid-Victorian, a highly successful essay in the picturesque. It is a pleasure to examine the conscious charms of these timbered fronts and to go through the tiny Leicester Square, half-genuine half-1850, into the churchyard and so to the church, 13th–14th century rehashed in the 19th. The Sidney chapel, although rebuilt early in the 19th century, has memorials going back to the 13th. Here is Sir Stephen of Penchester—who rebuilt Allington Castle—clad in mail. Also Sir William Sidney (but not Sir Philip who earned a resting place in Old St Paul's). Note tablet to Lord Gort, half-forgotten and heroic warrior of two World Wars—he was C.-in-C. of the B.E.F. in 1939. The Rectory is half hidden beyond the churchyard wall, a most elegant house with an 18th century face.

Penshurst is in the heart of exceptionally lovely country. It is a good centre for walks, upstream to Poundsbridge—where there is a spectacular magpie house dated 1593—and Smart's Hill—where one can eat well, into the Eden valley to Chiddingstone and Chiddingstone Hoath, and across the park to Leigh. Everywhere the gentle charms of the Weald are at their most delightful and refined.

PILGRIMS WAY—*a trackway across the county below the North Downs.*

The name is a 19th century whimsy. This is the survival of one of the prehistoric trackways which provided trade-routes through Britain. It runs from near Dover W. to the county boundary above Westerham (and on through Surrey and Hampshire to the metropolitan heart of prehistoric Britain on Salisbury Plain). At the Stour gap the eastward track divides, one—the more familiar—following the river to Canterbury, the other keeping below the escarpment of the Downs to reach Dover by a southern route. A parallel way follows the ridge of the Downs and can be followed in part. The Pilgrims

Pilgrims Way above Ryarsh

Way proper—signposted as such in Kent—is largely metalled now and makes a narrow byroad. The best parts for walking are from E. of Kemsing to Paddlesworth above Snodland, from Hollingbourne to Charing, and from Boughton Aluph to Canterbury.

PLAXTOL—*on greensand ridge N. of Tonbridge.*
A large, spreading and attractive village with many fine houses. From a distance it stands well on the side of the greensand hills with the church at a high point. This is a rarity, a new church of 1649 built in an archaic Gothic style—but largely altered in a Victorian restoration. There are pretty cottages nearby, a pub with an extraordinary name, and a first-rate and picturesque eating-house. To the W. the road

goes towards Ightham, giving a magnificent view over the Weald. The stone wall by the road is a boundary of Fairlawne —see Shipbourne—and a pretty path through the park leads to Shipbourne green.

At the foot of the steepish hill which leads down to the Bourne valley is Hyders, a factory for fine wrought-iron, with a half-timbered house beside it. The lane past this crosses the Bourne and then climbs to Old Soar, the rare and precious remnant of a knight's house—it belonged to Culpepers of course—of the late 13th century. The hall has gone—a handsome 18th century farmhouse occupies its position—but the stone-built solar remains intact. The solar itself stands on a vaulted undercroft with a chapel on the same level, and, behind, a projecting garderobe (lavatory). The building is in the care of the National Trust.

POSTLING—*in North Downs N. of Hythe.*
A lonely village with only a minor lane through it. It looks very pretty from the S. with the old cottages and the church spire set against the green swell of the Downs. The East Stour rises here, in a spectacular basin just below the Down, within sight of the sea, but turns W. to meet the Great Stour at Ashford. The church possesses one extreme rarity, an inscribed tablet recording the dedication in some unnamed year of the —presumably late—12th century. At The Pent, a farmhouse on the way to Stanford, Joseph Conrad lived during a productive period of his career.

POULTON—*in the North Downs behind Dover.*
Poulton? Never heard of it. That is reasonable, for the village, complete with church, disappeared long ago. A tablet marks the site of the church.

In the parish stood one of the major abbeys of medieval Kent, St Radigund's. This was a house of Praemonstratensian canons founded at the end of the 12th century. It had a large church with an unusual tower placed between nave and N. transept, together with the usual domestic buildings. At the Dissolution the abbey was left to fall into ruin and in Elizabeth's reign a house was made out of the frater while the tower became a gatehouse. Substantial remains survive in and around the farmhouse, and a public footpath offers good views. It would be nice if they could, like those of the other Kentish Praemonstratensian house at Bayham, be put into good order and made accessible to the public. They would make an attraction in this charming country.

QUEENBOROUGH—*on Sheppey.*
The Queen was Philippa, consort to Edward III, and the town was newly founded in this reign. It stood beneath the walls of a castle built according to entirely new principles to discourage attacks on the mouth of the Thames by raiders during the French Wars. Of this historic building nothing at all remains. It was dismantled during the Commonwealth and the last remains cleared away when the railway was built. Part of the earthworks can be seen near the station.

The town was politically important from its foundation until the Reform Act of 1832 deprived it of its two members. Mayor and Corporation continued up to the amalgamation of the island's three local authorities, and even then Queenborough, the smallest partner, managed to perpetuate its name in the new Borough of Queenborough-in-Sheppey. The town hall stands in the short decaying High Street. There is a gracious council chamber and the town regalia is magnificent. But Queenborough is rather a sad place, with nothing much to replace past glories. The church dates from the foundation of the town but has been much renewed. One or two houses nearby, including a handsome one with Nelson associations, set the right tone. At the end of the Street there is some maritime activity in the creek.

QUEX PARK—see *Birchington*.

RAINHAM—*now the easternmost part of Gillingham.*
On Watling Street, and there are still a few signs of former greatness in coaching days. But there is really nothing much for the visitor, apart from a fine ragstone church with one of the best of the characteristic Kentish church towers. There are exceptionally fine fittings and some interesting monuments, especially of 17th century.

RAMSGATE—*on Thanet coast.*
In the parish English history may be said to have begun with the landing of the Jutish horde and modern Christian history with the landing of St Augustine, both on Pegwell Bay where a modern note is struck by the hoverport. The former event is commemorated by the *Hugin*, a delightful and anachronistic replica of a Viking long-boat in which a crew of high-spirited Danes sailed to Kent to mark the fifteenth centenary of the arrival of Hengest, the latter by a Celtic stone cross erected by the roadside at Ebbsfleet.

As usual on Thanet the original settlement was inland, at St Lawrence where a Norman church stands in what is still essentially a village. Ramsgate itself came into its own with the craze for sea-bathing, and with the development of the harbour during the Regency. There are some reminders of these great days down by the harbour and in the terraces on the East Cliff. The town appeals most to admirers of Victorian achievements, both with domestic developments beyond the Front and with St Augustine's, a Roman Catholic church (now an abbey) which was Pugin's masterpiece and one of the supreme expressions of revived Gothic. The conspicuous and rather jolly lantern of St George's is earlier, from the 1820s, and infinitely more shallow—but a nice collector's piece nevertheless.

READING STREET—see *Stone-in-Oxney*.

RECULVER—*on N. Kent coast E. of Herne Bay.*
The twin towers are the principal landmark on Thames mouth. If they were not they would have followed the rest of one of the greatest Kentish churches to demolition.

Here the deep salt-water channel of the Wantsum reached the sea, and on the mainland shore the Romans built a stone fort in the 3rd century as part of a complex system to defend the Saxon Shore. Three and a half centuries later, when the fortress was much decayed, Egbert King of Kent encouraged the foundation of a Saxon abbey within the walls. Here arose one of the most elaborate and formal of early Saxon churches. To this was added, without falsifying the original concept, a pair of W. towers at the end of the Norman period. This great monument to the dawn of English Christianity was demolished, at the whim of the parson, in 1809, and only the towers were spared because they were useful for navigation. The melancholy and deeply evocative site is protected by the D of E.

RICHBOROUGH—*N.W. of Sandwich.*
The winding Stour skirts Richborough, giving a small idea of what the site was like when the wide channel of the Wantsum made it a peninsula. The Roman legions made this safe anchorage their base for the conquest of Britain in 54 A.D. and the site, growing ever more complex in its defences, remained the principal military base throughout the Roman occupation. In time a huge monument was put up, perhaps to celebrate the Conquest. The base of this is marked today by a huge cross-shaped mass of foundations. Much later the fortress was enlarged and strengthened to make it the biggest of the Saxon Shore forts.

The site was abandoned after the withdrawal of the legions, but St Augustine began his mission near here and perhaps through his influence a church was built within the walls.

Richborough was deserted in the Middle Ages and it was replaced by Sandwich, nearer the mouth of the Wantsum. It

Richborough

awaited the arrival of the Department of Public Buildings and Works which excavated the ruins and laid them out for public view. They form one of the most impressive monuments to the Romans in Britain. Standing among the shattered walls one looks across to the superb concrete towers of Richborough Power Station, a telling exercise in historical comparisons.

ROCHESTER—*on the lower Medway.*
This crossing of the tidal river must have been important before the Roman occupation. The Roman Watling Street crossed the river here and an important settlement grew up beside the ferry. A bridge must have followed quickly. The

Rochester Cathedral, West Door

Roman town was walled, and the line of the walls was followed by those of the medieval city which still remain in part. When St Augustine was firmly established in Canterbury he sent a mission to Rochester, and this became the second see in England with Justus as Bishop. His cathedral was built in 604, a little building occupying a site set across the west end of the present cathedral. This was rebuilt and enlarged, and the whole was destroyed by the first Norman Bishop Gundulf, who built one of the earliest of the Norman cathedrals in its place. Of this a square stumpy N. tower remains as well as part of the crypt. The present nave with its massive piers belongs to a 12th century rebuilding.

Rochester was inevitably the poor relation of Canterbury and for long lacked any attraction for pilgrims. Fortunately a saintly Scottish baker was murdered in Rochester while on pilgrimage at the beginning of the 13th century. The monks of Rochester acquired his body, and the fame of St William's shrine was sufficient to justify rebuilding the cathedral choir.

Rochester is small as cathedrals go, but it has much of real interest and beauty. The W. front is superb, even in decay. The door into the Chapter House is gorgeous work of the late 13th century. The crypt, like Canterbury's, is double, moving from heavy Norman to light Early English. Many good monuments, notably to Bishop John of Sheppey with contemporary colouring and to Bishop Walter of Merton, who founded Merton College at Oxford.

The precincts are pleasantly quiet in contrast to the hubbub of High Street. There are two medieval gates, College Gate from High Street where the sinister John Jasper lived (in *Edwin Drood*) and Prior's Gate. Minor Canons Row, also in *Drood*, is a pretty 18th century terrace. There were presumably Roman defences at the river crossing. Gundulf built one of the first stone castles here after the Conquest. This was greatly enlarged in Henry II's reign when the huge square keep was built.

Rochester Castle

King John besieged the castle in 1215 and wrecked one of the four corner turrets; the subsequent rebuilding can be clearly identified. The castle is well cared for and can be visited regularly. It affords fine views along the river and across to the Cathedral.

Rochester is a sad city at present. It is between stages, and the High Street, crowded with traffic but with many shops empty, is a melancholy sight. There are still many things worth a visitor's attention: the churches of St Nicholas (beside the cathedral) and St Margaret; Eastgate House, now the local museum; Watt's Charity, a triple-gabled stone house established for the entertainment of 'six poor travellers' about which Dickens wrote entertainingly in a neglected long-short-story; Restoration House, also with Dickens associations; Town Hall and Corn Exchange, the latter with an enormous clock over the street 'as if Time carried on business there, and hung out his sign'; La Providence, a little Victorian brick square marking a settlement of Huguenot refugees; St Bartholomew's, a hospital of Norman origin and with its original apsidal chapel. The list might go on a long time.

ROLVENDEN—*in Weald S.W. of Tenterden.*

A pretty town-like village with many weatherboard and brick houses. The church stands at a road junction in the most effective position. It is the big church of a prosperous late-medieval community getting its living out of cloth. It has one extraordinary possession, the big living-room squire's pew where the Gibbons worshipped after their fashion. The Gibbons, from whom the historian came, lived at Hole Place (gardens open). A nearer great house Maytham Place has vanished; Lutyens buried it within the huge bulk of Great Maytham, one of the biggest and most forbidding of his Georgian mansions.

The country around is very delightful. From the Benenden road a backward glance shows off the village well, and just beyond this vantage point is a well-restored post-mill.

Fairfield Church on Romney Marsh

ROMNEY MARSH

The 'Fifth Continent'. A large area, rising occasionally as much as eleven feet above sea-level, won over many centuries from the sea. Still one of the finest pastures in England and still producing the famous Romney Marsh sheep, it is becoming equally celebrated for corn and bulbs.

Reclamation was partly natural, through the building up of shingle banks by the tide and by the deposit of silt from the River Rother and its tributaries, partly artificial through the maintenance of 'walls', earth banks from Hythe to Dymchurch (Dymchurch Wall) and from Appledore to Romney (Rhee Wall).

Three marshes and a level comprise the area of Romney Marsh. The eastern half, up to the Rhee Wall, is Romney

Marsh proper; its capital is New Romney. Denge Marsh is the shingle area of which Lydd is the principal settlement. The alluvial level W. of Rhee Wall is Walland Marsh. This goes to the county boundary, and there is a detached marsh called Guldeford Level in Sussex.

ROTHER, RIVER—*a river of the Sussex border.*
Now almost entirely a Sussex river. It rises in the Weald near Rotherfield and flows through Robertsbridge, becoming the county boundary below Bodiam. It skirts Oxney, moving W. of the boundary near Rye and entering the sea at Rye Harbour.

Historically the Rother played an important part in the changing pattern of Romney Marsh. As the Limen it flowed in Roman times at the foot of the hills to Lympne. Later the course changed to the centre of the Marsh and it formed a wide estuary beyond New Romney. After the mouth was blocked by shingle in 1287 it moved to roughly its present course.

ROYAL MILITARY CANAL—*an artificial waterway designed as coastal defence during the Napoleonic Wars.*
The canal follows the line of the coast before the formation of Romney Marsh between Seabrook, between Sandgate and Hythe, in the E. and Pett in Sussex on the W. The canal is cut in a series of straight lengths with abrupt changes of direction designed to give the advantage in fire-power to the defender.

Today the Canal is an important factor in the drainage of the Marsh. Between Appledore and Warehorne the Canal and its N. bank belong to the National Trust. At Hythe it is used for boating.

ST MARGARET'S-AT-CLIFFE—*on E. coast between Deal and Dover.*
There are two distinct and separate communities, a very ancient settlement behind the cliffs and a modern seaside village residential rather than holiday. The cliffs here are the

White Cliffs near St Margaret's

steepest and finest in Kent, their chalk faces sheered off as if by a knife. Erosion is a problem and there are frequent falls. Sections of the magnificent cliff path from Dover to Kingsdown drop into the sea from time to time.

The old village is dominated by the church. This belonged to Dover Priory which may account for its splendour. It is the largest non-monastic Norman church in the county and is in the most lavish manner of the mid-12th century. Note the truly magnificent W. door, the wide nave and chancel, and the beautifully light interior, in contrast with most Norman buildings, due to a high clerestorey.

There is a little bay below the cliffs, almost Devonian in its steep approach and its enclosed feeling. The cliff top is largely built over, but to the E. the National Trust own a narrow strip of green. Just above this a tall obelisk in a fine position commemorates the work of the Dover Patrol in two World Wars.

Away to the S.W. there is a small isolated village, West Cliffe, consisting of little more than the flint church which comes from the late 12th century.

ST MARY-IN-THE-MARSH—*on Romney Marsh.*
Set in typical Marsh country, flat, intersected with dykes, with a few trees protecting the little settlement. The village is extremely small, just church, inn, farm and a few new cottages. The church is singularly perfect, an almost complete and little-restored building full of atmosphere. On the wall a memorial to E. Nesbit, who is buried in the churchyard. This supreme master of writing for children spent the last years of her life in a ramshackle house beside the little railway at St Mary's Bay.

The Bay has good sandy beaches, holiday camps and a miscellaneous collection of bungalows and holiday huts.

ST NICHOLAS-AT-WADE—*on Thanet, just S. of Thanet Way.*
The 'Wade' was a crossing of the Wantsum from the mainland to the island. St Nicholas's church tower is a grand landmark, massive 14th century work of highly individual design. The church stands squarely in the middle of the compact village with a brick 'Dutch' gable facing the porch, denoting the home perhaps of some homesick weaver-refugee in Elizabeth's reign. Despite outward appearances, St Nicholas is a largely late Norman church with sophisticated carving in the capitals. The village retains a certain 'frontier' character. It has some blemishes but does not fall far short of excellence.

ST PETER'S—see *Broadstairs.*

ST RADIGUND'S ABBEY—*see Poulton.*

SALTWOOD—*inland from Hythe.*
The parent parish of Hythe. A manor of the Archbishops with a palace which was strengthened during the invasion fears which followed reverses in the Hundred Years War. The great gatehouse—now the home of Lord Clark the art historian—is of this time, around 1385. In Becket's day Saltwood was held by Rannulf de Broc who supported the murderous knights against his lord, and the four knights used the castle as their base before moving on to Canterbury. The castle, with its great hall and battlement promenade, is open to the public on a number of summer days. A public footpath gives romantic glimpses of the walls and towers. The village is rather suburbanized but has a neat centre with a little green near the church. There are pleasant walks in the neighbourhood, taking in the curious 'mountain' of Summerhouse Hill, a detached chalk cone standing away from the escarpment of the downs. Sandling Park has a magnificent garden of rhododendrons and azaleas, open in the summer.

SANDHURST—*above the* Rother *valley.*
A typical Wealden village with a sizable block of houses on the high ridge and a detached community—but new houses are bridging the gap—around the church on a hill to the S. Beyond lie the marshes of the Rother and Kent Ditch, the county boundary, providing an agreeable muddy walk. This is a thoroughly pleasing place with no architectural highlights; even the church does not redeem its external promise.

SANDWICH—*on the mainland bank of the Stour.*
An ancient borough and Cinque Port. This is nearly Kent's answer to Rye; potentially a major tourist town but at present handicapped by an appalling traffic problem and by a mild

seediness. When there is a bypass, enthusiasts may breathe new life into Sandwich without destroying its unique quality.

Sandwich's prosperity came from its position at the southern mouth of the Wantsum channel and its greatness as a port declined with the silting up of the passage. Thereafter it revived as one of the major centres for cloth-making in Kent.

The visitor finds much to recall the great days: a rampart walk which follows almost the complete circuit of the town boundary, with accompanying town ditch for much of the way; two ancient gates, Fisher Gate on the quay and Barbican Gate at the tollbridge over the Stour; many fine old houses, especially in Strand Street; three medieval churches, St Clement's magnificent late Norman work with central tower and all the trappings of a Cinque Ports civic church inside, St Peter's decaying quietly and picturesquely in the heart of the town, St Mary's a strange fragment in perilous juxtaposition to the main street traffic; the Guildhall occupying one side of the market place, much altered but with a Tudor core. A haphazard stroll through the back streets will reveal much more. Outside the boundary, and just beyond the railway, is St Bartholomew's Hospital, now almshouses, with original 13th century chapel containing the canopied tomb of a knight, perhaps the founder. The Salutation, a Lutyens house near St Clement's, opens its Gertrude Jekyll garden to the public sometimes in the summer. The Stour winds erratically across flat ground with new industries and a great—and remarkably handsome—power station. Walks past the old mill lead pleasantly towards the sea, and a toll-road passes the famous golf-course—second only to St Andrew's—to the shore and the Sandwich Bay nature reserve.

SCOTNEY CASTLE—see *Lamberhurst.*

SEAL—*village on the A25 in Holmesdale.*

At present horribly disturbed by traffic but the motorway will

Seal Woods

bring relief. Travellers on the A25 see little of note except a fine timber-framed house on the crossing. The best of the village lies north, with a nice tangle of small streets and a noble tower to the church at the high point. One of the best of the characteristic Kentish towers. Seal Woods, straddling the main road, are glorious in autumn and there are more woods and brackeny commons to the south. Good walking country, with a famous viewpoint (National Trust) at One Tree Hill on the greensand ridge.

SEVENOAKS—*town on edge of greensand ridge.*
Now a superior commuters' settlement grafted on to an old town. The best of the old houses are to the south near the church and the school. The latter has a mixed bag of buildings, some elegant 18th century, a block in prison-like ragstone, and modern expansion on the edge of Knole Park. A public school founded by Sir William Sennocke in 1432. At the other end the town opens up with a green and the famous Vine cricket ground, one of the oldest in the country.

For most visitors Sevenoaks is Knole, one of the biggest and most fascinating houses in England. A palace of the Archbishops, built originally by Archbishop Bourchier in mid-15th century, 'acquired' from Cranmer by Henry VIII, given by Elizabeth to her cousin and later her Lord High Treasurer, Thomas Sackville, Earl of Dorset. The principal seat of the Sackvilles ever since. (Read *Knole and the Sackvilles* by Victoria Sackville-West, who was born here.) A complex mass of halls, galleries and courts, seemingly muddled at first acquaintance but revealing a kind of organic growth. 'A town rather than a house' said Virginia Woolf. Too many treasures for listing here, but look out for great hall, incredible silverware in King's bedroom, happy intimacy—after all that splendour—of the suite occupied by Lady Betty Germaine, delightfully nude figure of La Baccelli, mistress of the 3rd Duke of Dorset—an unusual heirloom!

Knole now belongs to the National Trust; the park is still Sackville property. In its way it is as fine as the house, a great estate—opened freely throughout the year—with some noble timber and lovely open glades in the landscape manner of the 18th century. Deer roam as freely as the visitors and more picturesquely.

SHEERNESS—*principal town of Sheppey.*
Great days—now past—as naval dockyard. Prosperity seeping

back as the old dockyard redevelops into industrial estate. A little remains in the central area—a drab church of 1835, a cast-iron clock-tower, some terraces facing the sea—to interest collectors of Victorian curiosa.

SHEPPEY—*island at mouth of Thames and Medway.*
The only link with mainland is modern lift-bridge with towers standing up nobly in the flat landscape. In effect there are three islands, Sheppey, Harty and Elmley—the last, accessible only by footpath over the pastures, is virtually uninhabited, a desert-island in Kent! (Mr Plomley, please note.) At present—and changes come fast here—the island has clearly defined areas, industry in N.W., suburbia in the middle, seaside bungalows and caravans on N.E., marshy emptiness towards the Swale.

See also *Eastchurch, Harty, Minster-in-Sheppey, Queenborough* and *Sheerness.*

SHIPBOURNE—*in northern Weald.*
An open village set with a jolly disregard for order around a large green. No outstanding houses but nothing displeases. A big church stands back, 19th century replacement of a rare Georgian building. The village makes a good centre for muddy footpath walks. To the N. is the great house Fairlawne in a landscaped park—footpath across it to Plaxtol. Fairlawne—now famous as a centre for racehorse training—was home of the Vanes, among them Milton's friend Sir Harry Vane, a republican who had the misfortune to survive the Restoration but not for long. Here was born, son of the steward, Christopher Smart, friend of Dr Johnson and brilliant off-beat poet. The house, with porticoed front facing the road, has gardens well worth a visit in the summer. Opposite the drive a pretty short walk to Ightham Mote begins.

SHOREHAM—*in Darent gap through the North Downs.* Although on the commuter line to London Shoreham remains incredibly unspoilt, although developers have tried their best —or worst. The hills rise sharply at either end of the main street and so the village is trapped most pleasantly in its little valley. The Darent here is the clearest stream in Kent and an extremely enjoyable walk follows it downstream for a mile. At the start, just below the bridge, there is a white house, home of Samuel Palmer who painted here the finest of his mystical interpretations of the Kentish scene. William Blake stayed with him here. Just E. of the village centre the church stands, the red brick tower with classical pinnacles belying its medieval origins. There are good things here, notably the rustic porch massive in oak and the rood screen, much the best in Kent and almost to be compared with those of Devon. It runs the full width of the church. From the churchyard there is a view to the hills where a white chalk cross commemorates Shoreham dead of two wars. A footpath climbs this hill and another crosses the facing hill within sight of Dunstall Priory where Lord Dunsany, poet, dramatist and unique humorist, lived.

SHORNE—*N. of the A2 between Rochester and Gravesend.* According to Dickens, who knew the place well in his Gadshill days, 'the fairest spot in the garden of England'—but that was long ago. He would not recognize much today, but the area immediately adjacent to the church is still largely untouched. The church is the best thing here, a bold flint building with the monument of a knight of the 13th century inside; also a font which is almost the twin of neighbouring Southfleet and doubtless from the same hand and chisel.

SISSINGHURST—*Wealden village N.E. of Cranbrook.* Hardly more than a single street with a pub or two, some neat cottages and a little Gothic-revival church. At Cranbrook

Sissinghurst Castle

Common to the N. lived Charles M. Doughty, traveller and master of English prose. On the edge of the village, Sissinghurst Court has charming gardens which are often open.

The fame of Sissinghurst derives from other gardens, those created by Victoria Sackville-West and Harold Nicolson during their long tenure of Sissinghurst Castle. After their death castle and gardens came to the National Trust and are open throughout the summer. The castle was never a fortress—although it once housed prisoners-of-war in the care of the historian Edmund Gibbon. A Tudor mansion was extended into a large palace which later fell into ruin. All that remains now is a gatehouse range, a tall central tower, and flanking garden cottages. There are relics of the Nicolsons in the tower and their library can also be seen. But the gardens are the thing. Not 'garden', be it noted. This is a chain of gardens, each conceived as a unit, and without too much of a master-plan. Allow yourself plenty of time to see it all without hurry. You need not fear starvation; teas are served in the oast.

SITTINGBOURNE—*on Watling Street E. of Medway towns.*

Not my favourite town, but it has some interest. The High Street between Central Avenue and church can be seen without excessive danger now that the M2 has syphoned off the worst of the heavy traffic. Here survive some old houses and an inn or two from the coaching days. South of the road there are quite good new municipal buildings and some of the better post-war developments.

N. of the main road is Milton Regis, a royal estate of Saxon times and for long a separate township. The Court House, a timber-framed building now a small museum, recalls past greatness; so does the enormous gaunt church, but everything else is in a sad state. At Murston there is a museum of barges.

SMALLHYTHE—*S. of Tenterden.*

Almost my favourite Kentish village. A very lovely setting on the edge of the Rother levels with the low swell of Oxney beyond. The little drainage channel, the Reading Sewer, was once an arm of the sea, and Smallhythe was the port of Tenterden with a modest shipbuilding industry and a useful income from port dues. There was a little dock alongside the harbour-master's half-timbered cottage by the quay. Although within the borough of Tenterden Smallhythe enjoyed a separate existence and in time acquired a little Tudor-brick chapel and a fine house beside it for the priest. All this was long ago. The sea channel silted up, and Smallhythe might have settled into permanent decay. But in 1900 Ellen Terry came here at the height of her fame and bought the harbour-master's house. She put new life into the village in which she played the unofficial role of squire. She left her house, together with the Priest's House, to the National Trust, and it remains a splendid memorial to Smallhythe's past, to the English stage and to a great lady.

SMARDEN—*Wealden village in Beult valley.*

Like other Wealden villages rather town-like in character, and showing signs of its prosperity in the Kentish cloth-trade. More fine houses here than any other place of comparable size in the county. Village and surroundings deserve the closest and most leisured study. The church is well placed in the heart of the community; a great building with impressive roof span. Neat two-arched medieval bridge over Beult at entrance to the village. No need to catalogue other attractions which are many; sufficient to say that for many this is the cream of Kent.

SNODLAND—*on the tidal Medway.*

Seen from the main road, noisy with cement and paper lorries, this looks nothing like the popular view of Kent. Garden of

England? more like the backyard! Superficial views are misleading. This is a nice little town with a good communal spirit and much antiquarian interest. One track of the Pilgrims' Way comes down to the river here and crosses it—but you can't—by an ancient ford. The church stands just at the crossing, a handsome building with some good Norman detail. Up the street there is a fine Kentish hall-house. There have been exciting archaeological finds here, but the cement works gobble up the land greedily. The downs are near, however, and at their most beautiful.

SOLE STREET—see *Cobham*.

SOUTHFLEET—*S. of A2 behind Northfleet.*
The trunk road acts as a cordon sanitaire and protects Southfleet from the industrial and residential blight of N.W. Kent. A scattered parish but the village itself has almost a model Kentish pattern, neat and compact. The church sits back at the end of a closed street with pretty cottages and an oast to complete the impression. The flint tower is a landmark. Inside is a 15th century font with carvings on its eight faces (see also Shorne). Sir John Sedley founded a school here in 1637 and this still forms part of the village school—a very rare survival.

On Watling Street at Springhead there have been excavations of a Roman settlement, perhaps the Vagniacae of the Antonine Itinerary.

SPELDHURST—*N.W. of Tunbridge Wells.*
In hilly country. The new building has been done fairly discreetly and nothing spoils the attractions of the old village, centred on a T-junction backed by the church. Some fine tile-hung and brick houses and a genuinely ancient inn. The old church was burnt down and rebuilt in respectable neo-Gothic style in 1871. Lush—and quite good—stained glass of the period.

STANFORD—*on Stone Street N.W. of Hythe.*

The village straggles and lacks cohesion, but there are some good houses. Interest is centred on Westenhanger, a large and largely ruined fortified house alongside the railway station. Highly romantic in decay. Westenhanger belonged to the Smythe family.

The Folkestone race-track is here.

STAPLEHURST—*in low Weald S. of Maidstone.*

The long straight main street follows the line of a Roman road from Rochester to the Wealden iron-workings. Large commuter-estates have been grafted, not too unsuccessfully, on to an ancient village. There is a pretty timber-framed range where the road rises to the church. In the church there is a low-side window and other interesting details, but no serious competitor to the S. door which has its original ironwork of the 12th century in which pagan symbols break through. At what was, before the railway, the northern boundary of the village, there is a memorial—now much overgrown—to Marian martyrs of Staplehurst.

Despite the modern sprawl there is some charming country around, especially in the valley of the Beult. Here, at Hawkenbury, the bridge still has, despite much reconstruction, a medieval core.

STOCKBURY—*in North Downs between Maidsone and Sittingbourne.*

Stockbury Valley is a deep dry valley in the chalk through which the main road runs and across its foot the M2 throws a magnificent concrete viaduct. The village lies to the N.W. On a high point, with views to the Medway Estuary, stands a fine flint church with a tall tower. Inside some good details have survived a drastic 19th century restoration. Between church and farmhouse there is a conspicuous artificial mound, the motte of an early Norman castle.

Arcades in the Choir, Stone (Dartford)

Very lovely country to the W. Here, above a soft green valley, is Queen Down Warren, a steep chalk bank famous for orchids and other wild flowers—A Kent Nature Reserve and readily accessible. (Take great care not to damage anything.)

STONE-NEXT-DARTFORD—*a desolate land of cement works active and abandoned beside the Thames.*

In this desert stands the 'Lantern of Kent', one of the few parish churches in the county which is of national importance. Don't be put off by the grubby exterior. A remarkably rich work of mid-13th century with luxuriant carving, especially in the wall-arcades of the choir. Exquisite polished shafts of the nave arcades and windows. The stone vault of the choir is modern. Faded wall paintings include a Murder of Becket.

Stone-in-Oxney

STONE-IN-OXNEY—*at the eastern extremity of Oxney.* The very steep slope—the cliffs of a lost coastline—and the church tower upon it are landmarks of Romney Marsh. A small and very charming village. In spring the roadside banks are full of daffodils. The church stands back beside a fine timber-framed hall house. The best feature is the tall 15th century tower, the most curious a stone standing in the base of the tower, on which a shallow sculptured figure of a bull shows faintly—almost certainly the altar of a Roman temple of the Roman soldiers' god Mithras.

A steep lane runs through the old cliff down to the Royal Military Canal, and another drops down to the creek, once an arm of the sea, at the Ferry Inn. A long low hill to the North here rises to a clump of trees. This is the site of Ebony chapel, in one of the lost villages of Kent. The chapel itself was taken down in the 19th century and reassembled at Reading Street.

STOUR, RIVER—*the principal river of East Kent.*
The main stream, the Great Stour, rises at Lenham and flows east to meet the East Stour at Ashford. The river turns abruptly here to Canterbury through a gap in the downs. At Stourmouth where the river used to enter the Wantsum it is joined by the Little Stour. Beyond Sandwich the Stour twists and turns for miles before it finds a way through the sand to reach the sea in Pegwell Bay.

Once famous as a trout stream, the Stour is now in grave danger of pollution.

STOURMOUTH—*E. Kent on River Stour.*
Here the river once entered the deep-water channel of the Wantsum. Plucks Gutter is a favourite place for anglers. The little village lies inland with a most interesting church at West Stourmouth. Here are Royal Arms of George III and many good details.

STROOD—see *Rochester.*

SUNDRIDGE—*in Holmesdale W. of Sevenoaks.*
The village does not show itself to advantage on the busy A25, although the Old Hall—antiques—is one of the best of Kentish hall-houses, restored to its original single-storey state in the thirties. A pretty church stands on a low hill S. of the road, looking as if it belongs more to Surrey than Kent.

N. of the road is Combe Bank, now a convent but occasionally open to the public. The 18th century house was restored at the end of the 19th century when Walter Crane, designer and book-illustrator, decorated the library in the height of fin-de-siecle fashion.

SUTTON-AT-HONE—*in Darent valley N. of Dartford.*
The village looks terrible from the main road; all the dirt of heavy industrial traffic thrown in its face. There is an unexpected haven in the midst of the squalor, the old house of St John's Jerusalem in its peaceful garden. Here was a manor of the warrior order of St John of Jerusalem, and a chapel survives from the days of the Knights. For the rest this is an unfussy house of the early 18th century, at one time the home of the Kent historian Edward Hasted and in our own time the home of that distinguished broadcaster and writer Sir Stephen Tallents. Owned by the National Trust now. The garden and chapel are shown on one week day throughout the year.

SUTTON VALENCE—*on greensand ridge S. of Maidstone.*
A minor Norman castle guarded the approaches to the Weald here, of which there are battered remains. Conspicuously on the hillside are the buildings of Sutton Valence School founded in Elizabeth I's reign. This is a pretty village, built on several levels with houses of five centuries terraced above the steep escarpment, all enjoying the spectacular views. The church is on the edge of the old village; it was rebuilt about 1825 and is rather a dull Georgian building.

SWALE—*the sea-water channel dividing Sheppey from the mainland.*
There is a big industrial area on the shore N. of Sittingbourne. Much of both shores is very lonely, and to the east beyond Faversham Creek is one of the emptiest parts of the crowded South-East.

SWANLEY—*on the London fringe.*
A new bypass—crossed at one point by a concrete footbridge of exceptional elegance—has brought some peace to Swanley and may in time enable an amorphous mass of houses to become a community. The first comprehensive school in Kent

is here. Swanley proper is in rural surroundings N. of the road. The modern town grew up around the railway junction where the lines to Chatham and Maidstone divide. There is little attraction here, but to the W. Kent and Greater London merge in an area of astonishing natural beauty. Lanes and tracks lead towards Orpington and the Darent Valley as quietly as if the Great Wen was a hundred miles away.

SWANSCOMBE—*an urban district on Thameside.*
The ancient village has all but disappeared under the weight of industry. Great towers mark the areas of active operation and to the S. the parish is carved up with old workings. In one of these were found the fragmentary remains of Swanscombe Man—strictly speaking Woman—who lived in a Kent infested with mammoth and woolly rhinoceros some 250 millenia ago. In such a time-scale the Saxon tower of the church seems almost new. There is more to be seen in the church than this, including the elaborate Jacobean tomb of Sir Anthony Weldon who was Clerk of the Kitchen to James I, a job sufficiently demanding to justify his worried expression. In the public garden beyond the church, beside the new Council Offices, is the 'Invicta' monument which commemorates the picturesque —if apocryphal—story of how the Men of Kent confronted William the Conqueror and won from him the confirmation of their ancient rights.

TEISE, RIVER—*tributary of the Medway.*
The principal river of the central high Wealden country. Rises near Bayham in Sussex and flows by way of Lamberhurst and Goudhurst and between Horsmonden and Marden to enter the Medway at Twyford Bridge, Yalding. An important stream but for the most part not a prepossessing one. Its prettiest course is between Lamberhurst and Goudhurst, reached by footpath from Lamberhurst Church. Small two-arch medieval bridge at Laddingford. The Teise and the Beult

are linked by a curious watercourse, perhaps artificial, called the Twist.

TENTERDEN—*small town in the eastern Weald.*
A borough and formerly a limb of the Cinque Port of Rye (see also *Smallhythe*). Its present elegant face was acquired during the town's prosperity at the height of the Kentish cloth trade when new houses were built and old ones had their faces lifted. The wide High Street is, a few blemishes apart, a wonderful example of the harmony produced by diversity; no two houses are alike, but they are all good neighbours.

The church (dedicated to St Mildred of Thanet; the town's name means the den—i.e. swine pasture—of the Thanet folk) stands on the highest point of the Wealden ridge, just behind the line of the High Street. Its best feature is the tower, which is the finest of its kind in Kent and the only one which offers a modest challenge to the great West Country Perpendicular towers. Note the unusual double West doors. Just behind the church there are good views over the Weald.

Although all the town houses deserve a glance there are no outstanding buildings. Beyond the central area, off the road to New Romney, is Hales Place which opens its gardens occasionally. The interest here lies in the survival of a walled Tudor garden with corner turrets and brick terraces and a pretty brick well house.

Tenterden has managed better than most the transition to the 20th century. Without losing its character it has become an excellent shopping centre, for quality as well as variety. Car-parking remains a problem and the lovely High Street with its fine limes is permanently disfigured by a double line of cars.

The old Kent and East Sussex Railway, once running from Headcorn to Robertsbridge, has hopes of a partial revival through the inspiration and practical efforts of enthusiasts. The line has been lost from Tenterden to Headcorn, but in

High Street, Tenterden

the other direction it still runs through delectable country along the valley of the Rother.

TESTON—*on the Medway W. of Maidstone.*
The river is crossed here by one of the medieval bridges, not perhaps the best but certainly contributing to one of the loveliest scenes in Kent. The picturesque ruins behind are not, as romantic imagination demands, monastic but the burnt-out remains of a mill. A neat wrought-iron village sign summarizes what Teston has to offer: the bridge, a cricket-ball factory and an honourable place in the fight against slavery. James Ramsay, vicar in the late 18th century, campaigned vigorously against the traffic. He is buried behind the church, a neat

undistinguished Georgian building pleasantly situated on a road which ends at the gates of Barham Court.

TEYNHAM—*on and to the N. of Watling Street, between Sittingbourne and Faversham.*

As usual the ancient settlement lies off the line of the Roman road, and the modern village grew up under the stimulus of the coaching age. Teynham is traditionally the original home of Kentish cherries and the best blossom is still to be seen in orchards surrounding the lonely church. This is a large building most memorable for a gorgeous modern Nativity in the East window, all rich blues and reds.

THANET—*the N.E. tip of Kent.*

Still technically an island, and this can be seen clearly on the approaches by Thanet Way and from Canterbury or Sandwich. A flat dome of chalk with ancient settlements at Minster, St Peter's, St Lawrence and St Nicholas. The urban masses along the coast came later when sea-bathers and trippers transformed the little fishing hamlets. Thanet still maintains a certain insularity and a liking for its own ways. See also *Broadstairs Margate, Minster-in-Thanet, Ramsgate, St Nicholas-at-Wade.*

THROWLEY—*in North Downs between Lenham and Faversham.*

A scattered downland parish with principal settlements, both small, at the church and the Forstal. The church, in delectable country, is a handsome building notable for its choir stalls with misericords and for monuments to Sondes and Harrises.

These latter came from Belmont, a large mansion towards Faversham with gardens occasionally open. Here lived the Lord Harris who was so powerful an influence on Kentish and English cricket in late Victorian times. At Throwley those depressed by the erosion of rural Kent, by motorways and

Channel Tunnels, Common Markets and pollution, will find a little of the authentic Kent.

THURNHAM—*below N. Downs N.E. of Maidstone.*
It is difficult to identify the village. One or two large houses and an inn on the Pilgrims Way. A surprisingly big church in a peaceful setting. Here lies Alfred Mynn, greatest of Victorian cricketers of Kent. Above the Pilgrims Way a narrow lane rises steeply and makes a hairpin bend around a high bank, the motte of a Norman castle. A few fragments of flint wall stripped of their facing stone, defy the antiquarian to interpret their original plan. The castle hill makes a fine playground with long views eastwards.

TONBRIDGE—*where the London–Hastings road crosses the Medway.*
The highest point of the navigable Medway and very much a riverside town. The Medway here divides to enclose a large flat island dedicated to sport and recreations. Above the bridge loom the shattered walls of Tonbridge Castle, a key fortress in the Conqueror's system and greatly enlarged in Edward I's reign. From the former survives the magnificent tall motte, from the latter an equally splendid gatehouse. The castle grounds are now a pleasure garden.

After this beginning the town is largely disappointing to visitors. A few good buildings, notably one half-timbered inn and a brick coaching inn, survive, but much of the new building in the High Street is commonplace and unworthy. There are better things in Bordyke and East Street (note the Portreeve's House). Behind here is the gaunt overlarge church. Only a little remains of the original school, founded by an Elizabethan Lord Mayor of London, Sir Andrew Judde, and administered by the Skinners Company, but the Victorian and later buildings add interest at the N. end of the High Street. Huge and horrible housing estates on the northern edge of the town.

Coldrum Stones, Trottiscliffe

There are still pleasant walks to be had, principally to the west by way of the river and its innumerable contributary streams. Life in Tonbridge has improved with the completion of the bypass which passes W. and S. of the town. Magnificent views from the approach road looking N.

TROTTISCLIFFE (*pronounced, believe it or not, Trosley*)—
at foot of North Downs between Maidstone and Wrotham.
A pretty and remarkably unspoilt village with a couple of inns, some unfussy cottages in brick and weatherboard, and little else. To the E., and detached from the village, is a little settlement around the church. Here was a manor-house of the Archbishops of which a few fragments remain. The church is

highly picturesque in setting and made memorable inside—in a not altogether desirable way—by a splendid and grotesquely out-of-scale pulpit; this is said to have come from Westminster Abbey and may have looked well there.

Beyond the church, approached by a rough track, are the Coldrum Stones (National Trust) which correspond roughly on the western bank of the Medway to Kits Coty on the East. Remarkable remains of a complex monument of the New Stone Age. A communal burial place, marked by a vast stone chest, with a ritual circle of great stones around it. The site has been affected by erosion and the monument is greatly confused, but it is still one of the most evocative places in Kent. Noble views eastwards along the downs, and ancient tracks (including the Pilgrims Way) make this the starting point of memorable walks.

TUDELEY—*Wealden village S.E. of Tonbridge.*
It stands on a low ridge above the Medway which here, at Hartlake Bridge, affords the start of most agreeable walks in both directions along the towpath. Tudeley itself hardly exists, just a farm, a few cottages and a little church approached through the farmyard. The great house hereabouts is Somerhill, a sandstone mansion much altered but substantially the house built for Lord Clanricarde at the end of Elizabeth's reign. The park and house were painted by Turner. The present owner lost his daughter in a tragic sailing accident, and she is commemorated most movingly in the East window of the church, a superb design by Chagall and surely the most astonishing sight in any village church in Kent.

Tudeley is associated with the neighbouring parish of Capel. Most of the population is at Five Oak Green which was a familiar place to cockney hop-pickers and the centre of the social and evangelical mission which served them. A tiny church is set in orchard country to the south; this has recently restored wall-paintings, illustrating the story of Becket who has associations—perhaps mythical—with the place.

TUNBRIDGE WELLS—*Wealden town S. of Tonbridge.* During the centuries of Tonbridge's medieval fame this was dense, virtually uninhabited forest. So it remained until Lord North, an unlovely member of James I's Court, returned home from Eridge Castle and discovered a chalybeate spring in the forest. Out of this chance came the fashionable spa, at first a temporary settlement of tents, then a little community focused on the Pantiles and the iron spring and with subsidiary settlements on the neighbouring heights of Mount Sion and Mount Ephraim.

Despite Regency and Victorian and later growth, some of the original Wells remains. The Pantiles, a little faded but still a notable arcade of shops which may again become elegant and fashionable. The Church of King Charles the Martyr (Charles I as seen by Royalists of the restored Stuart Court) is a plain brick box outside, inside a riot of baroque plasterwork. Above all the Common, which creeps into the heart of the town, breezy wooded uplands with outcrops of reddish-grey sandstone, lined with houses as varied in quality as in date and materials. From a later age comes the work of Decimus Burton, clumsy Gothic, rather grim terraces and crescents and the pretty Calverley Park, and from a later age still the modern civic buildings—for those who like that sort of thing.

When the attraction of the shops and the cinemas—among the best in the county—palls there are walks across the Common to Rustall Common with more rocky outcrops including the fantastic Toad Rock, and on to High Rocks, which are just over into Sussex. I don't much like paying to see natural phenomena but the High Rocks provide a playground, a living geological museum, and an archaeological site too, for here are thin remains of an Iron Age Hill Fort, a refuge

Next page: Medway Valley near Teston

perhaps for iron workers in the age immediately preceding the Roman conquest.

WALDERSHARE—*in hinterland of Dover.*
Hardly a village at all here, but the great park of the Earl of Guildford's estate with notable landscaping and trees. Waldershare is in the Kent coalfield but in this idyllic scene one would never know. A wild-life park is promised—or threatened—here.

WALMER—see *Deal.*

WALTHAM—*in North Downs S. of Canterbury.*
Until recently a tiny village in remote country. Some recent building, but still on the edge of some of the emptiest parts of Kent. Narrow lanes and footpaths lead through the Downs to Crundale and Wye. Nothing much of note in the village except the church, a typical Norman three-cell building with central tower. Plain interior except for admirable sedilia of 14th century.

WANTSUM—*the channel between Thanet and the mainland of Kent.*
At each end of the deep-water channel were Roman forts of Richborough and Reculver, and this was principal passage between the Downs and London River, saving the long haul around the North Foreland. Tide and silt gradually blocked the channel, which is now merely a drainage course through the flat country. Best seen from Thanet Way and at Sarre and, on foot, behind Minster-in-Thanet where the channel is accompanied by the medieval embankment of the Abbots Wall.

WAREHORNE—*on the edge of Romney Marsh.*
A very small village, picturesque but of minor antiquarian interest. R. H. Barham (Tom Ingoldsby) was vicar here. The

Royal Military Canal is just below the church, and here is a most agreeable canal-bank walk (National Trust) to Appledore.

On the main road to Tenterden, which misses the village, is a handsome mansion of the early 18th century, and a pub—The World's Wonder—with a witty sign.

WATERINGBURY—*in Medway valley S.W. of Maidstone.*
A straggling village with a through road too narrow for its traffic. Some new development of no quality whatever; the area opposite the church is enterprising and may please some—but not me. A poor church, restored almost to death. It does contain one unique bygone, the Dumb Borsholder of Chart: a borsholder is a parish constable, so a dumb borsholder is his wand of office—in this case a massive club very handy for breaking down the doors of suspects. Behind the church is Wateringbury Place, which opens its lovely gardens from time to time. Here is the rare survival of a formal water-garden with cascades and statuary. The house is a large red-brick mansion in the elegant symmetrical manner of the late 17th century. Down by the mill-pond, approached by a lane opposite the church, there is a pottery which invites and deserves visitors.

WEALD—*literally 'forest'.*
A wide band of country crossing the centre of Kent from east to west and continuing through Sussex and southern Surrey. The high Weald consists of rolling sand hills, e.g. between Tenterden and Tunbridge Wells, the low Weald takes in the central valley of the Medway and its tributaries. Dense forest until well into the Middle Ages with small clearings, the -dens which were pig runs and the -hursts, wooded hills. Much of the Weald was opened up as a result of the iron industry which flourished when the discovery of gunpowder stimulated a demand for iron for cannon and other weapons. A few of the

furnace and hammer ponds, which provided water-power for the industry, survive, notably at Cowden and Horsmonden. The Weald was also a centre for the cloth trade. Today an area of outstanding charm with handsome houses, prosperous farm land and some fine views.

WESTENHANGER—see *Stanford*.

WESTERHAM—*on Surrey border in Holmesdale.*
Suffers from excessive traffic problems on A25 trunk road (but M25 may rescue it in time). A small town built around a triangular green at junction of A25, the main East-West road through Kent, with road to Bromley and London. The best houses are on the main road and also up Hosey Hill towards Edenbridge. Large church with Surrey-type cap on tower; rare Royal Arms of Edward VI are inside. The town is associated with two famous men: James Wolfe, the conqueror of Quebec, who was born in the Vicarage and grew up in a gabled brick house—now Quebec House—at foot of hill (National Trust; Wolfe relics shown), and Sir Winston Churchill, whose country home for years was at Chartwell, to the S.E. Chartwell (NT) is the Trust's most popular property. Visitors who don't mind queues will see much evidence of the great man's presence, his studio and, especially, his magnificent garden with views over the Weald. Wolfe and Churchill both have monuments on the Green. Beyond the town to S.W. is Squerryes Court, home of Wolfe's friend John Warde and still occupied by Warde family (house shown). Very pleasant surroundings with to the S. some of the best walking country in Kent. Westerham Hill on North Downs is highest point in the county (824 ft).

Despite the traffic visitors soon discover that Westerham is a lively town with a strong sense of community. Shops (including a good bookshop) and two fine old coaching inns which stand facing one another in timeless rivalry.

WESTWELL—*just below North Downs to N.W. of Ashford.*
The village looks nothing much at a quick glance but deserves closer study. Attractions include (1) Westwell Woods, magnificent beech woods on the Downs, always lovely, incomparably beautiful in autumn (2) hospitable village inn, the Wheel, on the Green (3) watermill, now a house with a pretty garden beside the mill-race (4) church, dull outside but within spectacularly beautiful: stone screen, carved choir-stalls, finely carved sedilia.

WHITSTABLE—*N. Kent coast.*
A very long town, starting on the shell-strewn beaches of Seasalter and stretching eastwards beyond Tankerton to the pebbles of Swalecliffe. Had its finest hour in Roman times (when the oysters were at their best) and has never been the same since. There is a little atmosphere among the fishing sheds by the harbour but otherwise—unless you sail—rather dull and lacking in style. Old parish church, well to the S. near Thanet Way; beside it is the vicarage where W. Somerset Maugham spent an unhappy childhood. Quite good swimming, if the tide is right, at Tankerton and Swalecliffe.

WICKHAMBREUX—*on the Little Stour.*
Another 'top-twenty' village. Central green with pretty houses around and church beyond. Great weatherboard watermill at entrance to village. The general effect is quite delightful; details are slightly disappointing. Much of church's interest has been restored out of existence.

WINCHET HILL—see *Goudhurst.*

WINGHAM—*small town on Canterbury–Sandwich Road.*
Main body of the place contained within High Street between two pairs of sharp corners. Street of excellent houses which

repay careful study, starting with admirable early-18th century vicarage. Next is the very interesting church. There was a college of priests here, partly represented by the Chantry and the Black Lion Inn opposite, and this is a large collegiate church. Note choir stalls with grotesque carving of misericords, including a Green Man. Also dramatic rise of floor from West to East with high altar and its carved reredos at the highest point. Grand, or grandiose, monument to Oxinden family.

Several very satisfactory eating-houses here.

WITTERSHAM—*on central high point of whaleback Isle of Oxney.*

The gradual slopes deprive us of the expected distant views. Some new building but the village retains its character. Best is along lane past the church into Sussex across the River Rother, where there are several attractive houses. Typical Wealden church, wide and open and with lofty battlemented tower. At Stocks Green, on Rye road, is handsome postmill in good condition.

WOODCHURCH—*on high ground (comparatively—about 100 ft) E. of Tenterden.*

Land drops away to Shirley Moor and the Marsh. A large village around a green. Houses a mixed bag, but a handsome timber-framed cottage behind the green. For collectors of pub-titles The Bonnie Cravat opposite the church. The church itself is large (not of wood) with Bethersden marble shafts to pillars. The fine white smock-mill on the highest ground—a landmark—is getting shabby.

WOULDHAM—*on the tidal Medway.*

Not everybody's favourite picture-village, but a really concentrated effort might work wonders and a spirit of community is growing. The church is splendidly placed on the river-bank and its low battlemented tower is a familiar sight to the river traffic. The attraction here is the grave, on the south side, of Walter Burke, purser of Victory who stepped briefly into history when Nelson died in his arms. Downstream is Starkey Castle, visible from the road, a house incorporating some of the fabric of a manor-house of about 14th century. There are fine walks on to the downs, giving views across the Medway gap which reveal the fantastic contortions of the tidal river, and down to the splendid new Medway Motorway Bridge, and upstream the river bank is littered with the melancholy and strangely evocative ruins of old cement workings.

WROTHAM—*below North Downs at junction of A20 and A227 roads.*

On Wrotham Hill, just past the tall radio mast, the traveller from London sees for the first time the Promised Land. The village, almost townlike in its complexity, was an Archbishop's manor and also a coaching stage of some importance—hence fine Bull and other inns and scanty remains (behind the church) of Archbishop's Palace. Some very pretty houses, not quite ruined by the heavy traffic. If you like off-beat survivals from the past, note tablet in churchyard wall reporting a murder. Very handsome church, most of 14th century. Dedication is to St George, whose excellent modern statue looks out of a medieval niche in porch. The ancient—and modern—road passes so close to the West end that a processional way had to be made through the base of the tower. The country around has been too popular with commuters whose houses scar the sides of the hill and sprawl thickly to the south, but the National Trust has land to the east, beside the Pilgrims Way, in its safe grasp.

WYE—*town at head of Stour gap through North Downs.*

A place of great charm and character; inevitably it was chosen

View along the Downs, west of Wrotham

—having the necessary qualifications of beauty and poor road communications—as the site for an oil depot: the struggle continues. Birthplace of Archbishop Kempe who remembered his home town and founded a college of priests here in 1448. This later became a grammar school and later still formed the nucleus of the South Eastern College of Agriculture, now Wye College, the agricultural school of London University. Part of the original college is incorporated in the modern college and can be seen from the road. The buildings facing the road are in a safe academic tradition and very pleasing too. Behind, on the road to Olantigh, are more adventurous styles. The College gives Wye some of its atmosphere; it has attracted two bookshops—an unlooked-for luxury in Kent—and excellent eating-houses. The collegiate church is greatly transformed. A central tower fell in 1686, demolishing the chancel, and the building now ends abruptly in a shallow eastern apse. The nave is handsome work of about 1450. So far development of Wye has been contained between the river and the downs, and the new open-plan housing estate is a model of what can be done with just a little sensitivity and commonsense. The downs, with a chalk crown cut by students to mark the coronation of Edward VII, are famous for wild flowers. There are fine walks, notably one to Crundale by way of dry chalk valleys and bluebell woods.

YALDING—*at confluence of Beult and Medway.*
An ancient settlement in a classic position for Anglo-Saxon colonization. One of the most perfect of village streets, the vista closed at either end by a fortunate kink in the road. At the head stands a war memorial cross, a small strip of green with brick lock-up, and Cleaves, a 17th century house established as a school by a Carolean merchant. Here Edmund Blunden's father was Master, and Blunden grew up in Yalding, soaking in the traditions of Kent which became the raw

material of his verse. The street is flanked by two noble brick houses, one faces on to the road, the other reticent behind a high wall. The church is set back beyond the line of the road. At the foot of the street the road turns to cross the Beult by a long stone causeway of the 15th century. The bridge is best seen from the river bank behind the George Inn (buy a pint for the privilege of the view). Yalding Lees is a large open space between the Beult and the Medway. One area is given over to car-parking, and is hideously crowded in summer. Here the Medway is crossed by one of its finest medieval bridges, Twyford Bridge. The river Teise joins the Medway here and half a mile upstream is another ancient bridge at Laddingford. The towpath walk from Twyford upstream is particularly delightful.

At Benover, a hamlet on the Horsmonden road, there is an astonishing collection of houses, one—Normans—of major interest, and at least five others of exceptional charm. Also a picturesque inn, the Woolpack.

TOP TWENTY

There are no ugly villages, or ugly girls, in Kent, but some of both kinds are prettier than others. The following list is a personal selection of places which give me a particularly keen sense of satisfaction, because the buildings are of high architectural quality, or the plan is exceptionally pleasing, or the setting is lovely. Every reader will be able to match the list with one of his own making.

Appledore
Aylesford
Biddenden
Bishopsbourne
Boxley
Brenchley
Chevening
Chilham
Cowden
Elham
Goudhurst
Groombridge
Hernhill
Milsted
Penshurst
Smallhythe
Smarden
Stone-in-Oxney
Wickhambreux
Yalding

ANTIQUITIES

The principal evidence of the period up to the end of the Roman occupation of which considerable remains may be seen *in situ*.

Domestic
- Oldbury, rock shelters
- Lullingstone, Roman villa

Sepulchral
- Addington, long barrow
- Addington, The Chestnuts
- Aylesford, Kits Coty
- Aylesford, Little Kits Coty
- Aylesford, White Horse Stone
- Chilham, Jullieberrie's Grave
- Trottiscliffe, Coldrum
- and round barrows on Barham and Ringwould Downs

Defensive
- Bigbury, hill fort
- Canterbury, city walls
- Dover, Pharos
- Dover, Saxon Shore fort and port
- Lympne, Stutfall Castle
- Oldbury, hill fort
- Reculver, Saxon Shore fort
- Richborough, port, fort and amphitheatre
- Rochester, city walls
- Westerham, Squerryes hill fort

CASTLES IN KENT

Norman Castles

Chilham—keep only
Dover—many later additions
Eynsford—ruined
Folkestone, Caesar's Camp—motte
Malling, St Leonard's Tower—keep
Newenden, Castle Toll—motte
Rochester
Stockbury—motte
Sutton Valence—ruined
Thurnham—ruined
Tonbridge—with later additions

Medieval coastal defences

Cooling—fortified manor-house
Lympne—fortified manor-house
Queenborough—demolished
Saltwood—fortified manor-house

Fortified manor-houses, inland

Allington
Hever
Ightham Mote
Leeds—royal castle
Scotney

Post-Medieval Fortresses

Chatham—many forts
Deal—Henry VIII coastal fort
Dover, Western Heights—complex defensive system
Sandgate—Henry VIII coastal fort
Sandown—Henry VIII coastal fort, foundations only
Upnor—Queen Elizabeth fort with additions
Walmer—Henry VIII coastal fort with additions
and many Martello towers, best seen at Folkestone and Dymchurch

MONASTIC KENT

A list of the principal religious houses of which substantial remains can be seen today.

Augustinian

Bilsington
Minster-in-Sheppey (nuns)

Benedictine

Canterbury, St Augustine's
Canterbury, Christ Church (the Cathedral)
Davington (nuns)
Dover
Faversham
Malling (nuns)
Rochester, Cathedral

Carmelite Friars

Aylesford

Cistercian

Boxley

Cluniac

Monks Horton

Dominican Friars

Canterbury, Blackfriars

Franciscan Friars

Canterbury, Greyfriars

Military Orders

Strood (Templars)
Sutton-at-Hone (Hospitallers)
Swingfield (Hospitallers)
West Peckham (Hospitallers)

Praemonstratensian

Bayham
St Radigund's

A CHOICE OF CHURCHES

Saxon

Canterbury, St Martin's
Canterbury, St Pancras (ruins)
Dover, St Mary in the Castle
Lyminge
Minster-in-Sheppey
Reculver (ruins)

Norman

Barfreston
Minster-in-Thanet
New Romney
Patrixbourne
St Margaret's-at-Cliffe
Sandwich, St Clement's

Early English

Brookland
Hythe
St Mary-in-the-Marsh
Westwell

Decorated

Chartham
Cobham
Herne
Stone-next-Dartford

Perpendicular

Cranbrook
Maidstone, All Saints
Rainham
Tenterden
Wye

Post-Reformation

Groombridge
Mereworth
Otterden
Plaxtol
Tunbridge Wells, King Charles the Martyr

Gothic Revival

Chiddingstone Causeway
Northfleet, All Saints
Ramsgate, St Augustine's
Ramsgate, St George's

Modern

Little Chart
Wigmore

VIEWPOINTS

The reaction to views is subjective. Everyone responds in an individual way. For myself, I do not always want a view to be wide-ranging. Some of the loveliest extend for only a few miles; their quality comes perhaps from the absence of discordant notes, perhaps from a satisfactory frame in the foreground. I offer the following list purely as a selection from which the reader may test his own reactions.

Map references are to the O.S. one-inch sheets.

Birling Hill, looking E., S. and W. 171/671624
Boughton Monchelsea, from the churchyard looking S.E. 172/771498
Brenchley Hill, looking N. over Medway plain 171/681423
Brook, from the Devil's Kneading Trough 173/078454
Crockham Hill, view S. from Mariner's Hill 171/448514
Goudhurst, from the church 171/725379
Hernhill, view over Sheppey and Thames estuary 173/074598
Lympne, view of Romney Marsh from Shepway Cross 173/125350
Minster-in-Thanet, the view over Pegwell Bay, for its history and its violent contrasts 173/328654
Newington-next-Folkestone, looking W. 173/189386
Southborough, corner of Vauxhall Lane looking N.E. 171/576433
Stone-in-Oxney, view over Marsh 184/941266
Stowting Hill, looking S.W. 173/131396
Thurnham Hill, looking W. along the Downs 172/806583
West Peckham, view over Medway valley and Weald 171/641529
Wrotham, looking along the Downs from minor road 171/590597
Wye, from minor road above the Crown looking into Stour valley 172/974468

BOOKS TO READ

There is scarcely a limit to the literature of Kent. For those who surrender to the charms of this county, one book will lead to another until the end of time. And still the list grows. Never since the 18th century has there been so much original research among primary sources. For grim economic reasons not all the results will find their way into print, but they are increasingly deposited in libraries where they become accessible to students.

The following brief list offers a selection of books which will appeal to the general reader, together with some of the basic studies on which all subsequent writing has been founded.

Church, Richard. *Kent.* Originally published 1948; new edition 1972. A poet's warm appreciation of his adopted county.

Church, Richard, editor. *The little kingdom.* 1964. An anthology of writings about Kent.

Cox, J. C. *Kent.* 7th edition by R. F. Jessup. 1950. A 'Little Guide' giving brief notes on every parish.

Crouch, Marcus. *Kent.* 2nd edition 1967. A personal account of journeys through Kent.

Hasted, Edward. *History and topographical survey of the county of Kent.* 12 vols. 2nd edition 1797–1801. The classic history of the county.

Hughes, Pennethorne. *Kent.* 1969. A 'Shell Guide', particularly good on architecture and industry.

Jessup, Frank W. *Kent history illustrated.* 1966. Written for use in schools but of interest to every reader.

Newman, John. *North Kent and East Kent.* 1969. *West Kent and the Weald.* 1969. In the Penguin 'Buildings of England'. A searching examination of every important building in Kent.

Victoria County History of Kent. 3 vols. 1908–32. Incomplete but an invaluable general introduction.